THE
APOSTOLIC FATHERS
A New Translation and Commentary

THE APOSTOLIC FATHERS

A New Translation and Commentary

edited by Robert M. Grant

University of Chicago

Volume 1   An Introduction
by Robert M. Grant, University of Chicago

Volume 2   First and Second Clement
by Robert M. Grant, University of Chicago
and Holt H. Graham, Virginia Theological Seminary

Volume 3   Barnabas and The Didache
by Robert A. Kraft, University of Pennsylvania

Volume 4   Ignatius of Antioch
by Robert M. Grant, University of Chicago

Volume 5   Polycarp, Martyrdom of Polycarp, Fragment of Papias
by William R. Schoedel, Brown University

Volume 6   Hermas
by Graydon F. Snyder, Bethany Theological Seminary

THE
APOSTOLIC FATHERS

A New Translation and Commentary

Volume 2

First and Second Clement

by
Robert M. Grant
and
Holt H. Graham

THOMAS NELSON & SONS

Toronto   NEW YORK   London

PREFACE

These translations and commentaries are the work of Holt H. Graham of the Virginia Theological Seminary and Robert M. Grant of the Divinity School, University of Chicago. They have divided their responsibilities in the following way: Professor Graham has produced the translations of First and Second Clement and the commentary on Second Clement; Professor Grant has written the commentary on First Clement and the Introductory materials on both letters.

The Psalms are numbered in accordance with the Septuagint version of the Old Testament.

CONTENTS

PREFACE   v

CITATIONS AND ABBREVIATIONS   ix

FIRST CLEMENT   1

The Manuscripts and Early Versions   3
The Early Transmission   5
Modern Studies   9
The Principal Sources   10
Outline   14
Translation and Commentary   15
Quotations from Scripture   101
Scriptural Paraphrases and References   103
Allusions to Scripture   103
Selected Bibliography   105

SECOND CLEMENT   107

Introduction   109
Outline   111
Translation and Commentary   112
Quotations from Scripture   133
Allusions to Scripture   134
Selected Bibliography   137

CITATIONS AND ABBREVIATIONS

References to and citations from the Old Testament are usually made on the basis of the Greek version called the Septuagint (abbreviated LXX), and for this reason the meaning as well as the chapter and verse division will often differ from the Hebrew or the English translations.

The writings of the Apostolic Fathers are given the following abbreviations:

Barn.	Epistle of Barnabas
1 Clem.	Clement of Rome to the Corinthians
2 Clem.	2 Clement (sermon)
Did.	The Didache
Eph.	Ignatius to the Ephesians
Magn.	Ignatius to the Magnesians
Mand.	Hermas, Mandates
Mart. Polyc.	Martyrdom of Polycarp
Phil.	Polycarp to the Philippians
Philad.	Ignatius to the Philadelphians
Polyc.	Ignatius to Polycarp
Rom.	Ignatius to the Romans
Sim.	Hermas, Similitudes
Smyrn.	Ignatius to the Smyrnaeans
Trall.	Ignatius to the Trallians
Vis.	Hermas, Visions

In addition, the following abbreviations occur fairly often:

Ad Autol.	Theophilus, *Ad Autolycum*
Adv. haer.	Irenaeus, *Adversus haereses*
Ann.	Tacitus, *Annales*
Ant.	Josephus, *Antiquitates*
BCP	Book of Common Prayer
Bell.	Josephus, *Bellum Iudaicum*
Bibl.	Apollodorus, *Bibliotheca*

C. Apionem	Josephus, *Contra Apionem*
Chorogr.	Pomponius Mela, *Chorographia*
Clem. hom.	*Clementine homilies*
Diss.	Epictetus, *Dissertationes*
Ep.	*Epistles* (by various authors)
Exc. ex Theod.	Clement, *Excerpta ex Theodoto*
Geog.	Strabo, *Geographia*
H.E.	Eusebius, *Historia Ecclesiastica*
Ioh. comm.	Origen, *In Iohannem commentarius*
Iudic. hom.	Origen, *In Iudicum libros homiliae*
Leg.	Athenagoras, *Legatio*
Nat. animal.	Aelian, *De natura animalium*
Nat. hist.	Pliny, *Naturalis historia*
Od.	Homer, *Odyssey*
Orac. Sib.	*Oracula Sibyllina*
Paed.	Clement, *Paedagogus*
Pan.	Epiphanius, *Panarion*
PG	J. P. Migne, Patrologia Graeca
PL	J. P. Migne, Patrologia Latina
praef.	*praefatio* (preface)
Princ.	Origen, *De Principiis*
prol.	prologue
Rhet.	Aristotle, *Rhetorica*
Sel. in Ezech.	Origen, *Selecta in Ezechielem*
Str.	Clement, *Stromata*
Vit. Apollon.	Philostratus, *Vita Apollonii*

THE
APOSTOLIC FATHERS
A New Translation and Commentary

FIRST CLEMENT

THE MANUSCRIPTS AND
EARLY VERSIONS

There are only two Greek manuscripts of the letter of Clement (or, the Roman church) to the Corinthians. These are (1) the biblical Codex Alexandrinus, written in the fifth century and presented by Cyril Lucar, Orthodox patriarch of Constantinople, to the English crown; the text of Clement was first published at Oxford in 1633; and (2) the manuscript of the Apostolic Fathers copied in 1056 and discovered at Constantinople by Philotheos Bryennios, who published 1 and 2 Clement in 1875; the manuscript is now at Jerusalem. The latter manuscript is complete, while Codex Alexandrinus lacks a leaf of the text of 1 Clement (57:7–63:4). In addition, there are many quotations from 1 Clement in the *Stromata* which Clement of Alexandria composed at the end of the second century (see below).

1 Clement was translated into at least three languages, and we possess Latin, Syriac, and Coptic versions. (1) G. Morin discovered a Latin version of the second or third century in a Namur (Belgium) manuscript of the eleventh century and published it in the *Analecta Maredsolana* in 1894. (2) The letter is also found in a twelfth-century Syriac manuscript of the New Testament at Cambridge; Lightfoot discussed its readings in 1877 and R. L. Bensly translated it in 1899. (3) There are two Coptic versions. (*a*) A Berlin papyrus of the fourth century, lacking 34:6–42:2, was published by C. Schmidt in 1908. (*b*) A Strassburg papyrus of the fifth century, ending with 26:2, was published by F. Rösch in 1910.

All these witnesses deserve some credit, but the most important are the two Greek manuscripts. The Latin version

is generally accurate, but it contains some interesting alterations in 60:4–61:1, with the result that Clement and the
Roman church are depicted as those to whom God has
given authority. Harnack (*Sitzungsberichte der preussischen
Akademie der Wissenschaften*, 1894, pp. 261–273) argued
convincingly that these alterations in favor of papal authority were made either in the ninth century or, more probably, in the eleventh century when the manuscript was
copied. He also drew attention to other modifications, apparently intentional, in chapters 20 and 25; the notion of
"worlds beyond the ocean" in chapter 20, criticized by Photius (see below) among others, is removed, and the story of
the phoenix in chapters 25 and 26 is told in such a way as to
make it clear that the dead phoenix is reborn, for otherwise
the story would hardly point toward the resurrection.

THE EARLY TRANSMISSION

The First Letter of Clement to the Corinthians is one of the best-known writings of the Apostolic Fathers. Ignatius of Antioch probably alludes to it (along with 1 Peter) when he says to the Romans (3:1), "You have never envied anyone, you have taught others." The letter of Polycarp contains many allusions to its phraseology, as Lightfoot showed. It was highly valued at Corinth, as Hegesippus (Eusebius, *H.E.* 4, 22, 1) and Dionysius (*ibid.*, 4, 23, 11) indicate. Irenaeus summarizes the content of its introductory chapters and also provides a theological synthesis based on the whole letter (*Adv. haer.* 3, 3, 3, pp. 10–11).[1]

It is in the writings of Clement of Alexandria that 1 Clement is most frequently utilized. Clement refers to the letter as by Clement (*Str.* 1, 38, 5) or even by the apostle Clement (4, 105, 1) and also calls it "the letter of the Romans to the Corinthians" (5, 80, 1).[2] He already knew 1 Clement when he wrote his *Paedagogus,* for in it he derives a group of Old Testament quotations from the letter (*Paed.* 1, 91, 2; 1 Clem. 8:3). In the *Stromata,* however, he provides many more quotations and often explicitly indicates their source (noted with an asterisk below).

| *Str.* 1, 15, 2 | allusion to the canon of truth | 1 Clem. 7:2 |
| *1, 38, 5–8 | Old Testament exegesis | 1 Clem. 48:2–5 |

[1] His mention of fire prepared for the devil and his angels is not based on 1 Clement but comes from Matt. 25:41 (a passage he cites elsewhere). B. Botte's suggestion (*Revue des études augustiniennes* 2 (1956), 67–71) that he is using 2 Clement may be correct.

[2] Clement also calls Barnabas an apostle (*Str.* 2, 31, 2; 35, 5) as well as an *apostolikos* (2, 116, 3).

2, 65, 2	Old Testament exegesis	1 Clem. 50:6–7
2, 91, 2	synoptic quotations	1 Clem. 13:2
3, 100, 4	Old Testament quotation	1 Clem. 17:4
3, 107, 2	synoptic quotations	1 Clem. 46:8–9
4, 32, 2–33, 3	Old Testament quotations	1 Clem. 14:5–16:1
*4, 105–119	excerpts	1 Clem. 1:2–3; 9:2–4; 10:1, 7; 11:1; 12:1; 17:1–18:4; 21:2–22:8; 36:2; 38:2; 40:1; 41:4; 48:1, 6; 49: 4–5; 50:1–3, 6–7; 51:1; 52:2–4; 53:3–5; 55:4–6
5, 52, 3–4	Old Testament quotations	1 Clem. 46:2–3
*5, 80, 1	cosmology	1 Clem. 20:8
6, 64, 2	Old Testament exegesis	1 Clem. 48:2, 4

The last of these quotations is wrongly ascribed to Barnabas, perhaps because Clement otherwise never repeats his quotations from 1 Clement and he has already ascribed this passage to Clement of Rome in *Stromata* 1, 38, 5.

It is worth noting that there are significant passages which Clement does not employ. He does not make use of chapter 5 with its descriptions of Peter and Paul (elsewhere he makes no mention of their martyrdoms); he does not refer to the mythical phoenix (ch. 25); he omits any reference to the apostolic succession (chs. 42–44), for in his view the true spiritual authority is the "gnostic" (*Str.* 6, 106, 1);[3] and he omits references to voluntary exile and the virtues of the pagans (54:1–55:2). These omissions reflect his own lack of interest in the subjects discussed.

In later times at Alexandria the letter was still being read.

[3] See A. A. T. Ehrhardt, *The Apostolic Succession* (London, 1953), 134–135.

Origen twice ascribes 1 Clement 20:8 to Clement (*Princ.* 2, 3, 6, p. 121, 13–19 Koetschau; *Sel. in Ezech.* 8, 3, PG 13, 796C) and also summarizes the teaching of 1 Clement 55:1 (*Ioh. comm.* 6, 54, p. 163, 1–4 Pr.). Perhaps from Origen, Dionysius of Alexandria takes a quotation of 1 Clement 20:8 (*Ep. ad Hierac.* in Eusebius, *H.E.* 7, 21). The ninth canon *De poenitentia* by Peter of Alexandria is based on 1 Clement 5.[4] Finally, there is an allusion to 1 Clement 20:8 in Didymus of Alexandria (PG 39, 1596C–D).

Naturally this important letter was not preserved only at Alexandria. Eusebius of Caesarea summarizes it in his *Ecclesiastical History* (3, 7); Cyril of Jerusalem bases a passage in his *Catechetical Orations* (18, 8; PG 33, 1025B) on 1 Clement 25; Basil of Caesarea quotes 1 Clement 58:2 in his homily *On the Holy Spirit* (29; PG 32, 201C); and Epiphanius quotes 1 Clement 54:2 in his *Panarion* (27, 6, 4) —though he regards Clement as the author of the *Clementine Homilies* and the letters on virginity (26, 16, 8; 30, 15, 2). Both 1 and 2 Clement are found in the Codex Alexandrinus, copied by the scribe who wrote part of the Old Testament.[5]

In the West Clement was not so well known. Jerome provides three independent quotations from the letter in his biblical commentaries: 16:2 in his commentary on Isaiah (PL 24, 523C); 20:8 and 49:2 in his commentary on Ephesians (PL 26, 496A and 524C). It is clear, however, that 1 Clement was preserved at Rome, for John the Deacon (as Pope, either John I or John III) summarized chapter 43 and 44:1–3 in his *Expositum in Heptateuchum* (Lightfoot I, 187).

During late Byzantine times and in the Middle Ages, 1 Clement practically passed out of sight. Those who argued about Roman primacy preferred to use either the *Clementine Homilies* and *Recognitions* or the *Apostolic Constitutions,*

[4] M. J. Routh, *Reliquiae Sacrae* IV (2d ed., Oxford, 1846), 34, lines 12–19.

[5] H. J. M. Milne and T. C. Skeat, *Scribes and Correctors of the Codex Sinaiticus* (London, 1938), 91–93.

on the Greek side, or the Pseudo-Isidorian *Decretals*, on the Latin side. From the Greek point of view, Clement's orthodoxy left something to be desired, as Photius pointed out (PG 103, 408A); from the Latin point of view, his letter said nothing about papal primacy or even office.

It was not until 1633, then, that 1 Clement became available to Western Christendom through the edition which Patrick Young, librarian to Charles I, produced. And it was not until the rise of historical scholarship in the nineteenth century that its importance could begin to be adequately assessed.

MODERN STUDIES

There is no particular reason for discussing most of the commentaries on 1 Clement that appeared during the late nineteenth and early twentieth centuries. In general, they were far too strongly influenced by various theories of what early Christianity ought to have been, and therefore they were not often able to see what 1 Clement was. Partial exceptions, in my opinion, were provided by the commentary of J. B. Lightfoot, bishop of Durham, by the penetrating monograph of Wilhelm Wrede (*Untersuchungen zum Ersten Klemensbriefe*, Göttingen, 1891), and by the commentary, usually judicious, of Rudolf Knopf (Tübingen, 1920). Lightfoot's commentary suffers, as Harnack pointed out, from his theory that Clement was a collector and synthesizer of all sorts of miscellaneous bits of tradition; Wrede's work deals primarily with only two—though important—points (the Corinthian situation and the place of the Old Testament); and Knopf not only assumes that Clement should have reproduced the ideas of the major Pauline epistles, or some of them, but also interprets too much of his thought in relation to parallels from Hellenistic philosophy and religion. Furthermore, Knopf has a tendency to see liturgical parallels in passages which were probably used by later liturgists.

The most balanced treatment of Clement in modern times is that provided by Adolf von Harnack in his *Einführung in die alten Kirchengeschichte: das Schreiben der römischen Kirche an die korinthische* (Leipzig, 1929). Here we find cogent corrections of Lightfoot and Wrede, along with an invaluable introduction, a useful translation, and a not inconsiderable commentary. Since the appearance of Harnack's book nothing comparable has been published, although one may mention the English translation with notes by W. K. L. Clarke (London, 1937).

9

THE PRINCIPAL SOURCES

In addition to the quotations from the Old Testament and the references or allusions to New Testament books (listed below; some New Testament materials are probably derived from oral traditions), Clement seems to have made use of an anthology of Old Testament quotations. P. Prigent[1] has listed the principal criteria for discerning the use of such anthologies: (1) the presence of composite citations; (2) false ascriptions (e.g., a text of Jeremiah attributed to Isaiah); (3) textual variants independently shared by various authors; (4) a series of citations independently attested by several authors; and (5) the use of a series of citations for a purpose different from that for which they were collected. We may add that very vague source references point in the same direction. In other words, looking for an anthology is very much like tracking down the sources pasted together in a rather mediocre modern essay.

If we employ some of the above criteria in examining the Old Testament quotations in 1 Clement, we find the following passages in which an anthology (or several) may be present: 8:2–4; 13:1, 4; 14:4–5; 15:2–5; 22:1–8; 23:3–5; 26:2; perhaps ch. 27; 28:2; 29:2–3; 34:3, 6, 8; 50:4, 6; 52:2–4; and 56:3–15. W. Wrede[2] argued that passages such as these were cited from memory, and as long as we do not actually possess parallel passages in other contemporary authors, we must admit that he may have been right. For the sake of our hypothesis, however, we present the examples with a brief comment on each. (*a*) 1 Clement 8 even begins with a title, "on repentance," and his quotations start with Ezekiel 33:11 (no exact reference), continue with "good

[1] *L'épître de Barnabé I-XVI et ses sources* (Paris, 1961), 28.
[2] *Untersuchungen zum Ersten Klemensbriefe* (Göttingen, 1891), 64–67.

advice," and end with Isaiah 1:16–20 ("in another place"). (*b*) 1 Clement 13:1 contains a quotation of Jeremiah 9:23–24 (mixed with words from 1 Cor. 1:31—perhaps traditional?); in 13:4 there is a quotation of Isaiah 66:2 (no reference) which, to judge from its subject (the meek and gentle man) goes with the mixed quotations in 14:4–5—from Proverbs 2:21, Psalm 36:9, 38, and Psalm 36:35–37. (*c*) 1 Clement 15:2–6 contains a group of quotations on false piety ("lips" or "mouth") as contrasted with true piety ("heart").³ These come from Isaiah 29:13, Psalm 61:5, Psalm 77:36–37 and 30:19 (no break), and Psalm 11:3–5. Fifteen words are missing, because of homoioteleuton, at the end of Psalm 30:19 and the beginning of Psalm 11:3, in every witness to Clement's text except the Syriac version. We suspect that they were missing in his autograph and possibly in the florilegium underlying it, and that they were restored by an observant editor. (*d*) 1 Clement 22 describes God's call and his mercy, with a text composed of Psalm 33:12–18, run together with Psalm 32:10 (no reference). (*e*) 1 Clement 23 speaks of the coming of the Lord and contains an apocryphal "scripture" ("the prophetic word" according to 2 Clement 11:2–4) and another scripture consisting of Isaiah 13:22 and Malachi 3:1. The latter quotation suggests that Clement's source is messianic; for "the messenger of the covenant" it reads "the Holy One"; but it could be Jewish as well as Christian. (*f*) 1 Clement 26 contains mixed quotations from Psalms 28:7, 3:6, and 22:4 (all introduced by "somewhere") and a very inexact quotation of Job 19:26; the subject of all is resurrection. (*g*) Similarly, 1 Clement 28:3 provides a quotation from Psalm 138:7–9 ("the writing, somewhere"), which is quite different from the Septuagint readings but at one point (*katastrōsō*) comes close to the Hebrew. A man cannot escape from the omnipresent God. (*h*) 1 Clement 29 contains two passages on election, one from Deuteronomy 32:8–9 (no reference), the other ("in another place") beginning with Deuteronomy

³ See commentary on ch. 15.

4:34 but continuing from an apocryphal document. (*i*) 1 Clement 34:3 contains a highly mixed text (cf. Isa. 40:10; 62:11; Prov. 24:12) on the Lord's coming and its consequences (see *e* above). (*j*) In 1 Clement 34:6 a mixed quotation (Dan. 7:10; Isa. 6:3) describes the angels' worship of God; Clement seems to view this eschatologically, and the quotation in 34:8 from something like 1 Corinthians 2:9[4] may come from a florilegium section related to eschatology (see *e* and *i* above). (*k*) Similarly, the highly composite quotation in 1 Clement 50:4 (Isa. 26:20, an unidentified line, Ezek. 37:12) has to do not directly with "the visitation of Christ's kingdom," to which Clement relates it, but with resurrection (see *f* above), and that in 50:6 (no reference; Psalm 31:1–2) with forgiveness (see *d* above). (*l*) According to 1 Clement 52, God needs nothing but confession; but the Psalm quotations (7:18 or something similar, 68:32; 49:14–15; and 50:19) deal with the true nature of sacrifice.[5] (*m*) In 1 Clement 56 there is a collection of texts related to chastisement (*paideia*), introduced as "the holy word" (cf. 13:3); these consist of Psalm 117:18 plus Proverbs 3:12 plus Psalm 140:5, "and again it says" Job 5: 17–26 (it is possible that Clement, who clearly knows the book of Job, has added the last passage).

The word "somewhere" (*pou*) occurs in three of these references (15:2; 26:2; 28:2)—though we must admit that it also occurs in passages which we have not ventured to add to our hypothetical florilegium (21:2; 42:5). In none of these passages is there any precise reference to the speaker or writer of the biblical text (except to Job, 26:3, and "David the elect one," 52:2).

If there is such a florilegium, or collection of florilegia, we may perhaps suggest that it contained quotations on repentance (*a*) without false piety (*c*) and forgiveness (*d, k*), on sacrifice (*l*), on election (*h*) and chastisement (*m*), on

---

[4] On this text see Prigent in *Theologische Zeitschrift* 14 (1958), 416–429.

[5] Cf. Barn. 2:10 and Prigent, *Épître de Barnabé*, 43–46.

resurrection (f, k), and the coming of the Lord (e, i, j), and on rewards and punishments $(b, d,$ perhaps $j)$. Nothing in this florilegium is specifically Christian rather than Jewish,[6] and we may further suggest that it was created in Hellenistic Jewish circles.

[6] The words parallel to 1 Cor. 1:31 in 1 Clem. 13:1 certainly do not come directly from 1 Corinthians.

OUTLINE

Salutation
I. The situation (1:1–3:4)
  A. Proem: the occasion of the letter (1:1)
  B. The previous golden age at Corinth (1:2–2:8)
  C. The distressing present situation (3:1–4)
II. The nature of the Christian life (4:1–39:9)
  A. The evil consequences of jealousy (4:1–6:4)
  B. The necessity of repentance (7:1–8:5)
  C. The virtues of obedience, piety, faith, and hospitality (9:1–12:8)
  D. The cardinal virtue: humility (13:1–19:1)
  E. God's providential order and its peace (19:2–20:12)
  F. Man's moral response to God (21:1–22:8)
  G. The eschatological sanction (23:1–28:4)
  H. Holiness and its duties (29:1–30:8)
  I. The way of blessedness (31:1–36:6)
  J. Conclusion (37:1–39:9)
III. Solution for the Corinthians' problem (40:1–61:3)
  A. The divine origin of church order (40:1–44:6)
  B. The opposition of the wicked (45:1–46:9)
  C. The necessity of love (47:1–50:7)
  D. Practical conclusions about obedience (51:1–58:2)
  E. Solemn liturgical conclusion (59:1–61:3)
IV. The Church of Rome and the Church of Corinth (62:1–65:2)

14

First Clement

Salutation

The church of God which sojourns in Rome to the church of God which sojourns in Corinth, called and sanctified by the will of God through our Lord Jesus Christ: grace and peace from almighty God be multiplied for you through Jesus Christ.

Salutation–3:4. The first section of the letter consists of (1) a salutation from the church at Rome to the church at Corinth; (2) a well-constructed rhetorical proem setting forth the occasion of the letter in relation to the circumstances of both churches (1:1); (3) a laudatory description of the previous greatness of the Corinthian church (1:2—2:8); and (4)—with an "abrupt shift from classical style" (Jaeger)—a depiction of the present situation at Corinth (3:1–4). Like the epideictic proems of which Aristotle speaks (*Rhet.* 3, 14), that of Clement begins by assigning praise and blame. It clearly reflects his ability to write literary Greek at a high level (cf. a work which he knew, Heb. 1:1–4).

Salutation. The best analysis of this salutation is that provided by Erik Peterson ("Das Praescriptum des 1. Clemens-Briefes," *Pro Regno Pro Sanctuario . . . G. van der Leeuw* [Nijkerk, 1950], 351–357). He points out that the word "sojourning" was used of Jews and Christians in the Dispersion (Sir., prol. 34; Babylonian Talmud, Sanhedrin f. 112 b; Jas. 1:1; 1 Pet. 1:1). The expression "the church of God," however, reflects 1 Corinthians 1:2–3 (cf. 2 Cor. 1:1) and indicates that, like 1 Corinthians (1:3), this letter is a "catholic epistle" (cf. Dionysius of Corinth in Eusebius, *H.E.* 4, 23, 1). The expression "be multiplied" is also characteristic of Jewish writing. The Roman community is sending the Corinthians a letter of instruction based not on Roman primacy but on the spiritual gift of "exhortation" (cf. 1 Cor. 14:3; Rom. 15:4; Phil. 2:1–4)—compare 1 Corinthians 1:4, 10. (This explains why the letter can be regarded as inspired by the Spirit, 63:2; cf. 59:1.)

I. The situation (1:1–3:4)

A. Proem: the occasion of the letter (1:1)

1 It is because of a series of misfortunes and accidents that suddenly came upon us, beloved, that we have in our view been rather slow in turning our attention to the matters in dispute among you; that is to say, to the abominable and unholy schism,

---

The formula "grace and peace" is Pauline, while the expression "be multiplied" is found not only in Jewish writings but also in 1 Peter 1:2; Jude 2; 2 Peter 1:2 (perhaps from Jude), and in two examples based on 1 Clement (Polycarp, Phil. praef.; Mart. Polyc. praef.).

1:1. Something of the structure of Clement's proem can be indicated by a rather literal translation in sense-lines.

Because of the unexpected and repeated misfortunes and accidents
     which have come upon us,
we consider that we have paid attention too slowly
to the matters in dispute among you, beloved—
especially that matter alien from and foreign to God's elect,
the abominable and unholy sedition
   which a few persons,
     rash and self-willed,
       have kindled to such a degree of frenzy
   that the revered and famous and rightly-loved-by-all name—yours—
     has been seriously maligned.

(1) He explains the Roman church's failure to intervene earlier as due to sudden difficulties of some sort. Presumably these are not related to the persecution under Nero in A.D. 64, since (*a*) the description of the deaths of Peter and Paul in chapter 5 does not seem to reflect a situation *immediately* past (cf. 7:1), (*b*) two generations have passed since the time of the apostles (44:2–3), (*c*) the Roman emissaries have been Christians "from youth to old age" (63:3), and (*d*) Clement can call the Corinthian church "ancient" (47:6). Therefore they probably consist either of sporadic persecutions toward the end of Domitian's reign (A.D. 81–96), though little is definitely known about such persecutions, or of events about which we know nothing. (2) He intimates that it is the proper duty of the Roman church to intervene in the Corinthian situation, but he does not say why. (*a*) Certainly he has learned of a widespread report about the situation (47:7), perhaps from the presbyters rejected at Corinth (47:6); this report brings discredit upon Christians everywhere. (*b*) Certainly he expects the Corinthian community and its new leaders (ch. 54; 57:1–2) to accept the counsel of the Roman church (58:2) and, more precisely, to obey the words spoken by Christ through the

so alien and foreign to those called by God, which a few rash and
self-willed individuals have kindled to such a frenzy that your
good name, hitherto so well and affectionately known to all, has
come to be seriously maligned.

B. The previous golden age at Corinth (1:2–2:8)

2. For who, once he has visited you, does not hold in high
esteem the nobility and firmness of your faith? Or does not ad-

---

letter (59:1), which was written "through the Holy Spirit" (63:2).
The Roman emissaries are to report back on the results (64:1). (c)
It is a question, however, whether the relation of Rome to Corinth
reflects a primacy universally accepted or is based on the relation of
Corinth as a Roman colony to the capital city or is no different from
the relation of any important church to another in which trouble has
arisen. It is clear enough from the letters of Ignatius that the Roman
church had a primacy of honor; it is also clear that Ignatius himself
did not hesitate to give instructions to the churches of Asia Minor.
We conclude that 1 Clement is proof for a primacy of honor but not
certainly for a primacy of authority. (3) There is no mention of a
particular primacy of Peter (though Peter is given a place of honor in
5:4); instead, Clement lays emphasis upon apostolic-episcopal succession (chs. 42; 44). (4) Knopf p. 44 points out how fond Clement
is of double expressions (both nouns and adjectives) which are
practically synonymous; this is characteristic of Greek rhetoric. (5)
The vice for which the Corinthians (or "a few" of them) are blamed
is political in nature: "schism" or "revolt" against good order. In the
New Testament the word is used in this sense only in Mark 15:7 and
three times in Luke-Acts; it occurs fairly often in Josephus (e.g., in
regard to a Jewish revolt under Cumanus, *Ant.* 20, 105, 117) but,
above all, in Greek orations and histories written from a conservative
point of view. Given the fact that Clement regards Christianity as a
politeia (2:8; 54:4) and Christians as "citizens" (3:4; 21:1; 44:6;
51:2; 54:4), it is not surprising that he condemns sedition (2:6; 3:2;
14:2; 46:9; 51:1; 54:2; 57:1; 63:1) and those who revolt (4:12;
43:2; 46:7; 47:6; 49:5; 51:3; 55:1). He is also opposed to the
existence of "factions" (see commentary on 21:7). On the whole
subject see Jaeger pp. 12-13 and 113-114. (6) The "name" which
is consequently maligned is not only the name "Christian," though
this (cf. 46:7 and ch. 64) is involved, but specifically the reputation
of the Corinthian Christians, as the following sections show.

1:2–2:8. Clement now explains why the Corinthians' name has
been, and still is, so famous. His four generalizations represent a pro-
gression to a climax; particular examples follow in 1:3–2:8. The generalizations are based on the reports of visitors to Corinth.

mire your thoughtful and gentle Christian piety? Or does not broadcast your magnificent spirit of hospitality? Or fails to praise your complete and certain knowledge? 3. For you have acted impartially in all things, and conducted yourselves according to the laws of God, obeying your leaders and paying the elders among you the respect due them. You have instructed your young people in temperate and honorable thinking; women you have charged to do everything with a blameless and pure conscience, maintaining due affection for their husbands; and you have taught them also to observe the rule of obedience and to manage their households with dignity and all discretion.

Reaction of visitor	Adjectives	Noun
(1) high esteem	totally virtuous (cf. 2:8; 45:7; 57:3; 60:4) firmly established (cf. 6:2; 47:6)	faith
(2) admiration	sober (cf. 63:3; 64) mild (cf. 13:7; 21:7; 30:8; 56:1; 58:2; 62:2)	piety in Christ (cf. 11:1; 15:1; 32:4)
(3) proclamation	magnificent (cf. 9:1–2; 19:2; 60:1; 61:1; 64)	spirit of hospitality (cf. chs. 10–12)
(4) blessing (praise)	complete (cf. 44:2, 5; 55:6; 56:1) secure (cf. 33:3)	knowledge (cf. 36: 2; 40:1; 41:4; 48:5; also 44:2)

Jaeger pointed out that the verbs expressing the visitors' reactions are typically Hellenic, as are the adjectives describing the Corinthians' (Christian) virtues. It is interesting to note that the verbs, or forms related to their roots, all recur in Clement's section on the divine origin of church order (chs. 40–44). By "faith" he means primarily "fidelity to God." "Piety" (especially common in the Pastoral Epistles) refers to the Christian way of life as described in the rest of the letter. On "hospitality" see the commentary on chapter 10. "Knowledge," as Knopf p. 45 states, is something practical—knowledge of God's will and obedience to it. When these themes are taken up again (chs. 9–12), "obedience" is substituted for "knowledge."

1:3. In the golden age of the Corinthian church, Christians practiced impartiality (cf. 21:7; 47:3–4; 50:2; Jas. 2:1) and "walked by the ordinances of God" (3:4; 40:4; Lev. 18:3; 20:23; Jer. 26:4; Ezek. 5:6–7; 20:18; Lightfoot p. 10). They were subordinate to their rulers and paid suitable honor to the presbyters (elder men) among them. Here, as in 1 Peter 5:1–5 (cf. Polycarp, Phil. 5–6), the author is concerned not only with presbyters as such but with older men in general. The rulers or leaders of the church (for the expression see

2 You were all humble and free from arrogance, glad to obey
rather than command, to give than to receive. You were content
with the rations Christ provided and careful of them, diligently
storing up his words in your hearts, with his sufferings ever before your eyes. 2. Consequently a profound and rich peace was
granted to all of you, together with an insatiable longing to do
good, and a rich outpouring of the Holy Spirit came upon you.
3. You were full of holy counsel, and with zeal for the good and
in devout confidence you stretched out your hands to almighty
God, beseeching him to have mercy if in some way you sinned
inadvertently. 4. You strove day and night for the whole brotherhood, to the end that by compassionate mercy the full number

---

21:6; Heb. 13:7, 17, 24; Hermas, Vis. 2, 2, 6; 3, 9, 7) are due respect simply because they are rulers, for Clement uses the same word
in reference to non-Christian rulers in general (55:1), to Roman
rulers (5:7; 37:2–3; 60:4), to Jewish rulers (32:2), and to Egyptian
rulers (51:5). Similarly, the "rule" of which he speaks is Roman
(61:1); the "kingdom" is of God (42:3) or of Christ (50:3) or
Roman (61:1); and by the word "king" he refers to God (61:2) or
to an earthly ruler, either pagan (4:10; 12:2, 4; 55:1) or Jewish
(4:13; 32:2).

Here, as in 21:6, Clement follows the sequence rulers-presbyters
(older men)-young-wives. The sequence reminds us of the Pauline
wives-husbands-children-slaves (Col. 3:18–22; Eph. 5:22–6:1); but
Clement's list, unlike Paul's, seems to be arranged in hierarchical
order. The young are to have "measured" or "temperate" and "honorable" (three times in this paragraph; elsewhere 1:1; 47:5; 48:1;
cf. Phil. 4:8) thoughts; women are to have a pure conscience, to love
and obey (Col. 3:18; Eph. 5:22; 1 Pet. 3:1) their husbands, and to
manage their households well—in short, to be ideal Greek housewives
(Jaeger; cf. Tit. 2:5).

The golden age as here depicted becomes the norm for future behavior in 21:6–8, where again we find rulers-presbyters (older men)-
young-wives-children, and counsel for behavior like that described
here.

2:1–8. In the golden age the Corinthians possessed the Christian
virtue of humility (see commentary on 13:1—19:1) and were free
from arrogance (13:1; 14:1; 16:2; 21:5; 35:5). They obeyed (1:3);
they were more glad to give than to receive (Acts 20:35, a verse
echoed in 13:1 and 46:7); they were content with, and paid attention to, the spiritual provisions supplied by Christ (cf. Did. 10:3),
particularly his words (cf. Acts 20:35), which they carefully stored

of God's elect might be saved. 5. You were sincere and pure in heart, bearing no malice toward one another. 6. Every form of sedition or schism was detestable in your eyes. You grieved for the transgressions of your neighbors; you considered their short-comings your own. 7. You never regretted all the good you did, being "ready for every good work" [cf. Tit. 3:1]. 8. Having the adornment of an excellent and pious manner of life, you accomplished all things in the fear of him; for the commandments and just requirements of the Lord were engraved upon the tablets of your hearts.

---

up in their hearts; and they kept his sufferings before their eyes (probably an allusion to Gal. 3:1, as Knopf p. 46 points out). Jaeger noted that thus the words and the sufferings of Christ provide a model for Christians; we may add that such a conception is characteristically Pauline (cf. E. Larssen, *Christus als Vorbild* [Uppsala, 1962]).

According to Knopf p. 46, Clement reverses the New Testament idea that the Spirit produces, rather than is the reward for, moral behavior; his view is characteristic of "rational moralism." But where the pouring forth of the Holy Spirit is mentioned in the New Testament (Acts 2:17, 33; Rom. 5:5; Tit. 3:6) it is clearly related to apostles and others who are already acquainted with the Christian life. By "rational moralism" Knopf seems to mean "traditional Christianity."

The Corinthians prayed for forgiveness for involuntary sins (involuntary, since their will was set toward goodness) and also strove "day and night" (cf. 20:3; 24:3) on behalf of the whole Christian "brotherhood" (1 Pet. 2:17; 5:9). It has sometimes been supposed that the sequence day-night reflects Graeco-Roman rather than Jewish time telling; Paul says "night and day" (1 Thess. 2:9; 3:10; 2 Thess. 3:8); but the sequence day-night occurs five times in the Jewish-Christian Revelation (H. Hemmer, *Clément de Rome*, x). The Corinthians strove so that "the number of the elect" (59:2; cf. 35:4; 58:2) might be saved. Knopf claimed that Clement does not really have anything like predestination in mind, but W. C. van Unnik has shown (*Revue d'histoire et de philosophie religieuses* 42 [1962], 237–246) that the idea, based on Jewish and Christian eschatological sources, is related to Clement's conception of God's plan of salvation. The phrase he uses of the Corinthians as "ready for every good work" occurs in Titus 3:1 but may be proverbial (cf. 34:4). On the Christian *politeia* see commentary on 1:1. The expression "engraved upon the tablets of your hearts" comes from Proverbs 7:3.

C. The distressing present situation (3:1-4)

3 All renown and opportunity for expansion were given you—and then the Scripture was fulfilled, "The beloved ate and drank, he grew broad and waxed fat and began to kick." 2. From this there arose rivalry and envy, strife and sedition, persecution and anarchy, war and captivity. 3. Thus "the ignoble" rose up "against the honorable" [Isa. 3:5], those of no reputation against those of repute, the foolish against the wise, "the young against their elders" [Isa. 3:5]. 4. For this reason "righteousness" and peace "are far from you" [Isa. 59:14], since everyone has abandoned the fear of God and lost the eyes of faith, and neither walks in the way of his commandments nor conducts himself in accordance with his duty toward Christ. On the contrary, each follows the lusts of his evil heart because he has adopted that wicked and impious "jealousy" through which "death came into the world" [Wisd. 2:24; cf. Rom. 5:12].

II. The nature of the Christian life (4:1-39:9)

A. The evil consequences of jealousy (4:1-6:4)

4 For thus it is written: "In the course of time Cain brought to the Lord an offering of the fruit of the ground, and Abel

---

3:1–4. In order to explain how the golden age, so grandiloquently described in 1:2—2:8, came to an end, Clement ostensibly relies on a quotation of Deuteronomy 32:15. The question arises, Why this particular text? It may be that he had in mind the kind of proverbial wisdom expressed in a phrase like "prosperity brings forth *hybris*." At points like this, gnomic and biblical attitudes often overlap. Another possibility is suggested by peculiarities in the text as Clement reproduces it in verse 1. The concluding phrase is Deuteronomy 32:15b, the words *epachunthe* and *eplatunthe* occur in the next strophe, and the word *ephagen* occurs in the preceding one. The order is neither that of the Septuagint nor that of the Hebrew. It may be, then, that the phrase *ephagen kai epien* at the beginning is a deliberate allusion to 1 Corinthians 10:7, where the apostle Paul cited Exodus 32:4, 6.

4:1–39:9. The situation of the Corinthian Christians was so glorious, and the church grew so rapidly, that their decline can be ex-

brought of the firstlings of his flock and of their fat portions. 2. And the Lord had regard for Abel and his offering, but for Cain

---

plained only as a fulfillment of what God said about Jacob (LXX), "the beloved," in Deuteronomy 32:15. Elsewhere (59:1–2) Clement speaks of Jesus as God's beloved child; his idea about God's love for the Church is based either on God's love for Israel in the Old Testament or upon Ephesians, which he probably knew. The text in Deuteronomy goes on to say that "the beloved" abandoned the God who made him and departed from God his Savior. This is what Clement means by his picture of the rise of jealousy/envy, strife/sedition, persecution/anarchy, and war/captivity. The history of the schism has fulfilled the prophecy of Isaiah 3:5—and the gloomiest forebodings of Paul as expressed in 1 Corinthians.

ignoble against honorable	Isa. 3:5
no repute against reputable	Cf. 1 Cor. 4:10
fools against wise	Cf. 1 Cor. 4:10
young against elders	Isa. 3:5

(Paul himself alludes to Isaiah 3:3 in 1 Corinthians 3:10; has Clement followed his lead?) For other allusions to 1 Corinthians see the introduction.

The Corinthians do not know "the way of peace" (Isa. 59:8); they walk like blind men (Isa. 59:10); "righteousness is far off" (Isa. 59:14). The remainder of Clement's description is based partly on Old Testament language (without exact quotations), partly on the Hellenic, especially Stoic, norm of what is "suitable"—in this case, for Christ. The idea that through jealousy death entered the world is based verbally on Wisdom 2:24, though as Knopf p. 48 points out, in Wisdom the jealousy is the devil's, while Clement has the jealousy of Cain in mind (4:1–7).

According to Ziegler p. 77, the whole section of chapters 4–12 is dominated by the "jealousy" motif, but since it is explicitly mentioned only in chapters 4–6 (except for 9:1) it seems best to deal with these chapters separately. The theme has already been introduced in 3:1–2, where the origin of jealousy, envy, and strife has been ascribed to the spiritual prosperity of the Corinthians, and in 3:4, where it has been traced back implicitly to the jealousy of the devil.

Chapter 4 contains seven instances of the evil effect of jealousy (and envy) in Old Testament history, arranged in a rhetorically artistic pattern:

4:1–7 story of Cain and Abel (Gen. 4:3–8); "you see, brothers; jealousy and envy effected fratricide."
*4:8 "because of jealousy" (Jacob-Esau his brother)
4:9 "jealousy made" Joseph persecuted and enslaved (by brothers)
4:10 "jealousy forced" Moses to flee (because of fellow countryman)
*4:11 "because of jealousy" (of fellow Israelites; Aaron and Miriam)

and his offering he had no regard. 3. So Cain was very angry, and his countenance fell. 4. The Lord said to Cain, 'Why are you angry, and why has your countenance fallen? If you offered the sacrifice rightly, but did not rightly divide it, did you not sin? 5. Calm yourself. He will turn to you, and you shall rule over him.' 6. And Cain said to Abel his brother, 'Let us go into the field.' And when they were in the field, Cain turned on Abel his brother and killed him." 7. You see, brethren, that jealousy and envy result in fratricide. 8. Because of jealousy our father Jacob fled from the presence of his brother Esau. 9. Jealousy brought

---

4:12 "jealousy brought Dathan and Abiram alive into Hades" (rebelled against Moses, God's servant)

*4:13 "because of jealousy" David experienced "envy" (not only from strangers [Philistines] but also from the king of Israel)

These seven examples (arranged, as to form, a-b-a-b-a-b) generally combine the theme of jealousy (and envy) with that of exile (cf. 44:4, 6).

In chapters 5 and 6 similar motifs are present, also in seven statements:

5:2 "because of jealousy and envy" (the pillars were persecuted)
5:4 Peter, "because of unrighteous jealousy" suffered but was rewarded
5:5 "because of jealousy and strife" Paul was exiled but rewarded
*6:1 a great multitude suffered "because of jealousy"
*6:2 "because of jealousy" women were persecuted but rewarded
6:3 "jealousy has alienated" wives from husbands
6:4 "jealousy and strife" have damaged cities and nations

In the instances marked with an asterisk above, Clement clearly declines $z\bar{e}los$ (jealousy) as a neuter noun (also in 9:1; 14:1; 63:2), while elsewhere (3:4; ch. 5; 43:2; 45:4) he treats it as masculine. Whether this variety is related to content or to style (cf. Ziegler pp. 75–76) cannot be determined. It is obvious, however, that he is concerned with stylistic variation since the second set is arranged b (five times) plus a (twice); "jealousy and envy," presented in the first and the last Old Testament examples, recurs in the first Christian one, and is then replaced by "jealousy and strife" in the third Christian example and the last (cf. 3:2; 9:1).

It is possible that Clement's emphasis upon "jealousy" is partly based on his reading of the book of Acts, where Jewish attacks upon Christians are sometimes ascribed to this cause. The Sadducees were filled with jealousy (Acts 5:17); when "the Jews" saw crowds gathered to hear the word of God they were filled with jealousy (13:45); Jews at Thessalonica were jealous (17:5). But the motif means much more to Clement than it did to Luke. See also 1 Corinthians 3:3: "jealousy and strife."

about the near-fatal persecution of Joseph and his reduction to servitude. 10. Jealousy made Moses flee from the presence of Pharaoh, king of Egypt, when he heard his fellow tribesman say [Exod. 2:14], "Who made you a judge or assessor over us? Do you mean to kill me, as you killed the Egyptian yesterday?" 11. Because of jealousy Aaron and Miriam were excluded from the camp. 12. Jealousy brought about the swallowing up of Dathan and Abiram in Hades because they rebelled against Moses, the servant of God. 13. And it was because of jealousy that David not only incurred the envy of Gentiles, but was persecuted even by Saul, king of Israel.

4:1–13. This chapter contains seven examples of the consequences of jealousy as depicted in the Old Testament; as Klevinghaus p. 67 points out, in listing such examples Clement always follows the sequence of the biblical accounts. He introduces his first and most famous example—Cain and Abel—with the formula "it is written," which he frequently employs (ten instances). His quotation from Genesis 4:3–8 is close to the ordinary Septuagint text except that he twice omits "Lord" from the expression "Lord God," perhaps because of Hellenistic influence. After the quotation he gives a summary typical of the synagogue sermon. Then he briefly states the consequences of jealousy when Jacob fled from his brother Esau (Gen. 27:41–45), Joseph was persecuted and brought into slavery (Gen. 37; by his brothers, though Clement does not say so perhaps because he has already mentioned brothers twice and is passing now to nonfraternal examples), Moses was denounced by his fellow countryman (Exod. 2:14–15; on the text see below), Aaron and Miriam were lodged outside the camp (Num. 12; only Miriam is mentioned, but perhaps Clement adds Aaron because the greater priest Jesus suffered "outside the camp," Heb. 13:12–13), Dathan and Abiram went down alive into Hades (Num. 16:33) because they rebelled against God's servant (cf. 43:1; 51:3, 5; Num. 12:7), and David was envied by foreigners (Philistines) and persecuted even by Saul, who was king of Israel.

For Clement's style in this chapter see the commentary on chapters 4–6.

In quoting Exodus 2:14, Clement changes the Septuagint text from "who made you a ruler and judge over us?" to "a judge or assessor"—apparently recalling Luke 12:14, where many New Testament manuscripts have been influenced in turn by the Septuagint.

Cain's sin is attributed to jealousy in the Jewish(-Christian) *Testament of Benjamin* 7 (cf. V. Aptowitzer, *Kain und Abel in der Agada* [Vienna, 1922], 14–15).

5 But let us pass from ancient examples to those who contended for the faith in our own time. 2. It was due to jealousy and envy that the greatest and most righteous pillars (of the Church) [cf. Gal. 2:9] were persecuted and contended to the death. 3. Let us set before our eyes the good apostles. 4. There was Peter, who because of unrighteous jealousy endured not just one or two but many hardships, and having thus borne his witness, went to the place of glory he deserved. 5. Because

---

5:1-4. Now that he has completed his register of "ancient examples" from the Old Testament, Clement turns to the "athletes" (cf. Polyc. 1:3; 2:3; 3:1) of modern times; he follows the usual rhetorical custom of turning from past to present, and mentions "noble" (a favorite Greek word, three times in chs. 5–6, also 25:3; 54:1; cf. Mart. Polyc. 2:1–2; 3:1) examples of those who "because of jealousy and envy contended unto death." The first of these were the "pillars" (James, Peter, and John in Gal. 2:9; cf. C. K. Barrett in *Studia Paulina . . . J. de Zwaan* [Haarlem, 1953], 1–19), whom Clement identifies as "the good apostles"—not only Peter but also Paul. He regards not Jerusalem (as in Galatians) but Rome as the center of Christian life. Since medieval times it has occasionally been argued that Peter was not a martyr at Rome, but Clement seems to believe that he was (especially in light of the context in ch. 6).

Of Peter, Clement knows that he (1) "endured sufferings" (Stoic, cf. Sanders pp. 14–17) three or more in number, (2) "bore witness" (Sanders pp. 21–22), and (3) went to "his due place of glory" (Sanders pp. 31–34). It cannot be denied that Clement looks upon Peter as equivalent to a Cynic-Stoic hero. At the same time, he is definitely coordinating Peter as an example with the Old Testament heroes (ch. 4) who were victims of jealousy. His ideas are basically Jewish and Christian, only secondarily Stoic and Cynic. Furthermore, we may ask with Morton Smith (*New Testament Studies* 7 [1960-61], 86–88) where he gets his information about Peter's struggles. Smith points out that in Acts the word "jealousy" (*zēlos*) occurs only twice (5:17; 13:45); once it explains the persecution of Peter and other apostles and once it explains a controversy with Paul and Barnabas. It seems rather likely that Clement has relied on Acts here (three examples of Peter's suffering occur in Acts 3; 5; 12). We should incline to explain Peter's going to the due place not so much in relation to Acts 12:17 ("he . . . went to another place"; contrast Acts 1:25)—though Clement may possibly be echoing these words—as in relation to his theme of the athlete's reward.

For other probable echoes of Acts see below; also 2:1 (13:1; 46:7); (14:1; 42:3–4).

5:5-7. Paul too suffered because of "jealousy and envy," and

of jealousy and strife, Paul showed how to win the prize of patient endurance: 6. seven times he was in bonds, he was ban-
ished, he was stoned, he became a messenger (of the gospel) in
both east and west, and earned well-merited fame for his faith;
7. for he taught righteousness to the whole world, having
traveled to the limits of the west; and when he had borne his
witness before the rulers, he departed from the world an out-
standing example of patient endurance.

Clement provides examples to prove his case. He was in bonds seven
times (perhaps Clement took five examples from Acts and added two
from the epistles, but all may come from Acts); he was put to flight
(cf. 2 Cor. 11:32–33; Acts 9:25, etc.); and was stoned (2 Cor. 11:25;
Acts 14:19). Like the Cynic-Stoic hero Heracles-Hercules, he was a
worldwide "herald" (Sanders pp. 13, 30–31), making his proclamation both in the east and in the west presumably in fulfillment of the
prophecy in Malachi 1:11: "From the rising of the sun to its setting,
my Name is great among the Gentiles" (cf. Ignatius, Rom. 2:2). The
statement that "he earned well-merited fame for his faith" is purely
Hellenic, as is the mention of his reaching "the limits of the west." In
the Palestinian Psalms of Solomon (17:12) "the west" means Rome;
but for the Roman Clement, as for Strabo (*Geog.* 2, 1, c. 67; 3, 5, 5,
c. 169), "the limits" to the west or of the inhabited world are Cadiz
and the Pillars of Hercules (cf. Philostratus, *Vit. Apollon.* 5, 4: "the
limit of Europe"). In Clement's view, then, Paul visited Spain as he
had planned to do (Rom. 15:24–28), and afterward "gave his testimony" or "was a martyr" before the Roman authorities ("rulers" as in
37:2–3; 55:1; 60:4–61:2), thus leaving the world and, like Moses,
being "assumed" into heaven.

The word Clement uses in speaking of Paul's endurance is *hypogrammos*, a pattern or norm which in the letter is provided by Paul
or by Christ (16:17) or by the Creator (33:8). It is thus close to a
"sign" given by God (11:2; 12:7; 25:1; cf. 51:5) but is also an "example" (*hypodeigma*) to be imitated (5:1, Israelites and apostles;
6:1, Roman martyrs; 46:1, Old Testament saints; 55:1, Gentile rulers;
63:1, all of these).

The way in which he depicts both Peter and Paul owes a good
deal to the Cynic-Stoic ideal of the perfect athlete (for this see
Sanders pp. 8–34).

With G. Bornkamm (*Sitzungsberichte der Heidelberger Akademie
der Wissenschaften*, Philos.-hist. Klasse [1961], No. 2, 33) it should
be pointed out that nothing in this section of 1 Clement, or any other,
reflects acquaintance with the autobiographical sections of 2 Corinthians. He knows only one letter of Paul to the Corinthians.

6 To these men who lived holy lives there was joined a great multitude of the elect, who through jealousy endured many outrages and tortures and so became illustrious examples for us. 2. Because of jealousy women were persecuted as Danaids and Dircae, in which roles they endured dreadful and unholy outrages, and having reached the goal in the race of faith, they received the noble prize, and this despite their physical weakness. 3. Jealousy estranged wives from their husbands, and nullified the saying of our father Adam, "This is ncw bone of my bones and flesh of my flesh" [Gen. 2:23]. 4. Jealousy and strife have overthrown great cities and uprooted great nations.

B. The necessity of repentance (7:1–8:5)

7 We write such things to you, beloved brethren, not only to

6:1–4. The men mentioned in chapter 5 lived as holy citizens. Clement is very fond of the word *hosios* for "holy" (adjective six times, adverb eight times, noun four times), and he also thinks of Christianity as a "citizenship" or "way of life" (verb five times, noun twice). With them was gathered a great multitude of the "elect" (cf. 1:1; also common)—presumably during Nero's persecution, when, according to Tacitus (*Ann.* 15, 44, 6), a *multitudo ingens* was put to death. Clement ascribes their "outrages and tortures" to jealousy; he may have in mind the fact, mentioned by Tacitus, that Christians informed against one another. From the multitude he turns to give examples of women who suffered; cf. 55:3 and the examples cited by Knopf p. 53. The women were persecuted as "Danaids and Dircae." Here we probably have an allusion to mythological plays, given in the Colosseum, in which the martyrs were put to death (Tacitus, *Ann.* 15, 44, 7). From Suetonius (*Nero* 11, 2; 12, 2) we know that Nero was fond of a kind of bloody realism in his plays; and the daughters of Danaus were given to the victors in a gymnastic contest, while Dirce was bound to the horns of a bull (cf. Apollodorus, *Bibl.* 2, 1, 5; 3, 5, 5). Knopf p. 53 rightly retains the manuscript reading (though perhaps *hōs*, "as," could be added). Lightfoot pp. 32–34 lists emendations which seem quite unnecessary, including "women, maidens, slave-girls" (so A. Dain in *Recherches de science religieuse* 39 [1957], 355–358).

Clement then provides two rhetorical generalizations on the effects of jealousy: (1) it has estranged wives from husbands (the quotation from Gen. 2:23 is not very apt), and (2) it has overthrown great cities and nations (cf. Catullus 51:15–16 on the effect of *otium*; for the sequence women-cities-suffering from gossip, cf. Sir. 28:17–19).

7:1–8:5. Like the apostle Paul (1 Cor. 4:14), Clement is "writing"

admonish you but also to remind ourselves; for we are in the same arena and the same conflict faces us. 2. Therefore we should give up empty and futile concerns, and turn our attention to the glorious and solemn rule and standard of our tradition. 3. Let us attend to what is good and pleasing and acceptable in the sight of our Maker. 4. Let us fix our gaze on the blood of Christ and realize how precious it is to his Father, for it was poured out for our salvation and brought the grace of repentance to the whole world. 5. Let us survey all the generations and learn that in generation after generation the Master gave "an opportunity for repentance" [Wisd. 12:10] to those who are willing to turn to him. 6. Noah preached repentance, and those who heeded him were saved. 7. Jonah proclaimed impending destruction to the Ninevites, but they repented of their sins and by their supplications propitiated God and received deliverance even though they were aliens from God.

---

and "admonishing" his "beloved" correspondents; but he is also thinking of the Roman situation in which, in the past at least, jealousy has obviously played a part (chs. 5–6). The way to overcome jealousy is to concentrate attention upon Christian tradition and its declaration of what is good, pleasing, and acceptable before God (cf. 1 Tim. 2:3; Ps. 132:1). It is likely that Clement has Psalm 132 in mind because in it (*Ecce quam bonum*) the unity of brothers is compared to sacred ointment poured on Aaron's head; he himself turns to mention the blood of Christ (see below) and the "grace of repentance" consequent upon it.

Chapter 7 contains examples of forgiveness resulting from repentance; chapter 8 contains Old Testament quotations on the same subject.

7:1–7. Continuing the athletic metaphor of chapter 5, Clement says that Corinthians and Romans are in the same arena (metaphorical also in Epictetus, *Diss*. 4, 8, 26) and face the same contest (so Phil. 1:30). Therefore we should abandon "empty and futile" cares (the adjectives occur both in LXX and in Plutarch; Lightfoot p. 35) and come to "the rule and standard of our tradition" (cf. 19:2; 51:2; Polycarp, Phil. 7:2 [based on Clement])—the tradition found in the Old Testament and handed down from Christ and the apostles (Knopf p. 55 against Lightfoot p. 36). We should see what is "good and pleasing" (Ps. 132:1) and "acceptable" before God (cf. 1 Tim. 2:3), gazing upon the blood of Christ, a theme which is very important for Clement (12:7; 21:6; 49:6; cf. 55:1), since this blood is "precious" (1 Pet. 1:19), was poured out for our salvation, and won the "grace of repentance" for the whole world. Knopf pp.

8 The ministers of the grace of God through the Holy Spirit spoke of repentance, 2. indeed the Master of the universe himself spoke of repentance with an oath: "As I live, says the Lord, I do not wish the death of the sinner, but his repentance," and he added this gracious decision: 3. "Repent, O house of Israel, of your iniquity. Say to the sons of my people, Though your sins reach from earth to heaven, though they be redder than scarlet and blacker than sackcloth, yet if you turn to me with your whole heart and say, 'Father,' I will give ear to you as to a holy

---

55–56 criticizes this "universalism" but neglects its presence in John 6:51 (cf. John 3:16). On the meaning of "grace" here see Torrance p. 46.

Repentance, or the call to repentance, was not given solely through Christ's blood; Clement proceeds to "survey all the generations" in order to show that an "opportunity for repentance" (Wisd. 12:10) was offered in Old Testament times. Knopf p. 56 criticizes Clement's "rationalism and moralism" and his lack of emphasis on election; but this passage seems to be close to Matthew 12:41–42. Clement begins with Noah's preaching of repentance, for which see Josephus, *Antiquities* 1, 74 and the rabbinic references cited in S. Rappaport, *Agada und Exegese bei Flavius Josephus* (Vienna, 1930) 93, n. 53. Jonah similarly foretold destruction to the Ninevites; they repented, prayed, were forgiven, and gained salvation—though they were aliens, that is, Gentiles (cf. Eph. 2:12).

8:1–5. The ministers of God's grace (cf. Heb. 1:7, angels as ministering spirits; 1 Pet. 1:10–11, prophets predicting grace and inspired by the Spirit of Christ) spoke through the Holy Spirit about repentance; thus Clement turns from examples to quotations. The first of them, referred to "the Master of the universe" himself, begins with a verse close to Ezekiel 33:11, but continues with some "good counsel" which cannot be identified but is partly based on Isaiah 1:18; it may come from an apocryphal version of Ezekiel used by Christians. The quotation from Isaiah 1:16–20 which follows is very close to the Septuagint text. God's establishment of a share in repentance is proved by the oath "as I live" in the first quotation. For a similar oath see 58:2.

The basic reason for assuming that Clement is using the apocryphal Ezekiel (on which cf. M. R. James in *Journal of Theological Studies* 15 [1913–14], 236–243; K. Holl, *Gesammelte Aufsätze zur Kirchengeschichte* II [Tübingen, 1928], 33–43; C. Bonner, *The Homily on the Passion by Melito Bishop of Sardis and Some Fragments of the Apocryphal Ezekiel* [London, 1940], 183–190) is that Clement of Alexandria ascribes to Ezekiel something very close to the last part of the quotation (*Paed.* 1, 91, 2). Various scholars have

people" [Ezek. 33:10 ff., paraphrased]. 4. And in another passage he speaks thus: "Wash yourselves and become clean; put away the wickedness from your souls before my eyes; cease to do evil, learn to do good; seek justice, deliver the wronged; uphold the rights of the orphan and do justice to the widow; and come, let us reason together, says the Lord: Though your sins be as purple, they shall be white as snow; though they be as scarlet, they shall be white as wool; and if you are willing to heed me, you shall eat the good things of the earth; but if you are not willing and do not heed me, the sword will devour you; for the mouth of the Lord has said this" [Isa. 1:16–20]. 5. So wishing to have all his beloved participate in repentance, he established it by his almighty will.

C. The virtues of obedience, piety, faith, and hospitality (9:1–12:8)

9 Wherefore let us be obedient to his sublime and glorious purpose, and as suppliants of his mercy and goodness let us fall

---

suggested that the Alexandrian derived them from his Roman namesake; if so, he could have added a mention of Ezekiel simply because the quotation in 1 Clement does begin with something from that prophet. Alternatively, both Clements are using an anthology of quotations. On the question of anthologies see the introduction.

9:1–12:8. After the examples (ch. 7) and texts (ch. 8) which point to repentance, Clement provides a new series of examples (9:3–10:2; chs. 11–12) and texts (10:3–6) on the rewards of faithful obedience (9:3–4; 10:1) and faith and hospitality (10:7; 11:1; 12:1). Like the examples in chapters 4–6, these are very carefully arranged.

> 9:3 Enoch, found righteous in obedience, was translated
> 9:4 Noah, found faithful through his ministry, proclaimed
> 10:1 Abraham was found faithful in his being obedient
> 10:2 through obedience he went forth to inherit the promises
> 10:7 because of faith and hospitality a son was given him
> 11:1 because of hospitality and piety Lot was saved (11:2 sign given)
> 12:1 because of faith and hospitality Rahab was saved (12:7 sign given)
> 12:8 both faith and prophecy exemplified in her

The sequence Enoch-Noah-Abraham already occurs, with reference to faith, in Hebrews 11:5–10; Lot and his wife are mentioned in Luke 17:28–32 (after Noah, 17:26–27; cf. 2 Pet. 2:5–7, Noah-Lot); and the sequence Abraham-Rahab is found in James 2:21–25 (Rahab

down before him and turn to his compassion, forsaking fruitless
toil together with strife and the jealousy that leads to death.
2. Let us fix our attention on those who have served his sublime
glory to perfection. 3. Let us take as an example Enoch, who because he was found righteous in his obedience was translated
and never saw death. 4. Noah, because he was found faithful in
his service, proclaimed renewal to the world, for through him
the Master saved the animals that entered peacefully into the
ark.

10 Abraham, who was called the friend, proved faithful in

---

also in Heb. 11:31); compare also Sir. 44:16–19: Enoch-Noah-
Abraham.

The sections dealing with Abraham, Lot, and Rahab are summarized by the fourth-century theologian Ephrem Syrus in his little
work *De humilitate* 33 (*Opera graeca* I, 310).

9:1–4. A rhetorical transition leads from repentance (chs. 7–8) to
the Christian virtues required by the Corinthian situation (chs. 9–12).

Action	*To what related*
let us obey	God's magnificent (see commentary on 1:2) and glorious purpose
let us fall down before him as suppliants of	his mercy and goodness
let us turn to	his compassion (cf. 18:2; 20:11; 56:1)
forsaking	fruitless toil (typically Hellenistic, Knopf p. 57)
	strife (nine times)
	jealousy leading to death

It is difficult not to suppose that Clement's examples are inspired by
a similar list in Hebrews 11:5–7, since (1) there the names occur in
the same order; (2) there they are followed by Abraham, as in 1
Clement 10, and finally by Rahab, as in 1 Clement 12; and (3) 1
Clement 36 proves that Clement knew Hebrews. In Hebrews these
persons are listed as heroes of faith, not of obedience; but (1) Clement shares with James (2:14–26) the view that faith without works
is dead, and (2) he speaks of the fidelity of Noah, Abraham, and
Rahab.

In Jewish thought Enoch was ordinarily given the epithet "righteous" (Knopf p. 58). Noah foretold a new age (*Orac. Sib.* 1, 195;
for the word *palingenesia* in this sense cf. Matt. 19:28), and it was
anticipated in the harmony of the animals in the ark (cf. 20:10).
The idea that an age came to an end with the flood is clearly set
forth in 2 Peter 2:5; 3:6.

10:1–7. Abraham (as in Heb. 11:8), the friend of God (cf. 17:2;

that he obeyed the words of God. 2. For he went obediently
from his land and kindred and from his father's house, with the
result that by leaving a little country and a weak clan and a
small household he became the heir of the promise of God. 3.
"Depart from your country and from your kinsfolk to the land
which I shall show you. And I will make of you a great nation
and I will bless you and I will make your name great, and you
shall be blessed. And I will bless those who bless you and curse
those who curse you and all the tribes of the earth shall be
blessed through you" [Gen. 12:1–3]. 4. And again when he parted
from Lot, God said to him, "Lift up your eyes and look from the
place where you now are to the north, the south, the east, and
the west, for all the land which you see I will give to you and
to your seed forever. 5. And I will make your seed as the dust of
the earth: if you can count the dust of the earth, then your seed
will be counted" [Gen. 13:14–16]. 6. And again it says, "God
led Abraham out and said to him, 'Look up to heaven and count
the stars, if you can: so shall your descendants be.' And Abraham
believed God, and it was reckoned to him as righteousness"
[Gen. 15:5–6]. 7. Because of his faith and hospitality a son was
given him in his old age, and in his obedience he offered him to
God as a sacrifice on one of the hills God showed him.

Jas. 2:23), follows Enoch and Noah among Clement's examples of
faithful obedience. First he summarizes; then he gives an explicit
quotation of what "God says to him" (Gen. 12:1–3, LXX). The
promise to Abraham was given again when he was parted from Lot
(Gen. 13:14–16), and once more when "it [scripture] says"—Genesis
15:5–6 (with a few omissions for the sake of Greek style). Because
of Abraham's "faith and hospitality"—presumably virtues absent at
Corinth (H. Chadwick in *Texte und Untersuchungen* 79 [1961],
281–285)—he was given a son in his old age after he "entertained
angels unawares" (Gen. 18:2–3; Heb. 13:2), and in obedience he
offered his son as a sacrifice to God (Gen. 22; Heb. 11:17; Jas. 2:21).
   Clement is obviously following Hebrews (which he knew) or
James or perhaps a traditional Jewish pattern which lies behind both.
His collection of examples is presumably related to the Corinthian
situation, however (Chadwick). "Faith and hospitality" recurs in
12:1; "hospitality and piety" in 11:1. Hospitality, already emphasized
in 1:2, is a Christian virtue in Hermas, Mandates 8, 10, and ideally
characteristic of bishops in Similitudes 9, 27, 2.

11 Because of his hospitality and piety, Lot was saved from Sodom when all the country round was judged with fire and brimstone, when the Master made it clear that he does not abandon those who set their hope on him but delivers to punishment and torment those who turn away from him. 2. Of this Lot's wife became a symbol, for when she had gone out with him and then changed her mind and disagreed, she was made a pillar of salt that stands to this day. This was to make it clear to all that the double-minded and those who doubt the power of God fall under condemnation and become a warning for all generations.

12 Because of her faith and hospitality Rahab the harlot was saved. 2. For when the spies were sent out to Jericho by Joshua the son of Nun, the king of the country found out that they had come to spy out the land and he sent out men to intercept them

---

11:1–2. Lot was saved (Gen. 19:17, 22) from Sodom when the whole countryside (Gen. 19:25) was judged through fire and brimstone (Gen. 19:24). He was saved because of his hospitality (10:7; 11:1) and piety, for the Master (see commentary on 7:5) does not abandon those who set their hope on him (cf. 12:7; 16:16 [Ps. 21:9]; 59:3) but delivers to punishment and torture (cf. 6:1–2; 17:5; 45:7; 51:2) those otherwise inclined (47:7, of non-Christians).

Lot's wife went with him (Gen. 19:16), but she was not in agreement with him (she did not believe, Wisd. 10:7; she was too much concerned about Sodom and did not think that God would destroy it, Josephus, *Ant.* 1, 203) and therefore became a pillar of salt "to this day" (cf. the passages just mentioned; also R. M. Grant, *Miracle and Natural Law* [Amsterdam, 1952], 182–183). The double-minded who have doubts about God's power incur judgment and thus provide a warning to others. See the rabbinic parallels in S. Rappaport, *Agada und Exegese bei Flavius Josephus* (Vienna, 1930), 93, n. 53.

Double-mindedness is mentioned (verb, noun, adjective) fifty-eight times in the Shepherd of Hermas; in 1 Clement, only three times (here and in 23:2–3). As for the other writings of the Apostolic Fathers, it occurs three times in 2 Clement, once in the Didache and in Barnabas; never in Ignatius or Polycarp. It is obviously a concept characteristic of Jewish Christianity.

12:1–8. Another example of "faith and hospitality" (see 10:7) is provided by Rahab, an example of faith in Hebrews 11:31 and of faith and works in James 2:25. The copyists of various manuscripts, like those of the manuscripts of Hebrews 11:31, differ as to whether she was a prostitute (Alexandrinus; Clement of Alexandria) or was

so that when they had been captured they might be executed.
3. So the hospitable Rahab took them in and hid them in an up-
stairs room under stalks of flax. 4. When the king's men learned
of it they said, "The men who are spying on our country came to
you; bring them out, for so the king commands," she answered,
"The men whom you seek did come to me, but they left immediately and went on their way," and she pointed in the wrong
direction. 5. Then she said to the men, "I am absolutely certain
that the Lord God has handed over this country to you; for the
fear and terror of you have fallen upon all the inhabitants. So
when it comes about that you take over, save me and my father's
household." 6. So they said to her, "It shall be as you have said.
When you learn that we are approaching, gather together under
your roof all your family, and they shall be preserved; for all
that are found outside the house will perish." 7. And they also
gave her a sign, that she should hang a piece of scarlet from her
house, thus showing that it was by the blood of Christ that re-
demption was going to come to all those who believe and set
their hope on God. 8. Observe, beloved, that not only faith but
prophecy as well is found in this woman.

D. The cardinal virtue: humility (13:1–19:1)

13 So then, brethren, let us be humble and put away all pre-

---

called a prostitute (Jerusalem; Latin, Syriac, Coptic versions). The
story about Rahab and the spies of Joshua is freely based on the account in Joshua 2:1–18. Clement departs from the text in a manner
reminiscent of Josephus (*Ant.* 5, 1–15. 26), whose books, published at
Rome, he may have known and surely had heard of. Direct quotations become indirect, and vice versa, and the story becomes much
clearer for a Greek reader. Oddly enough, in 12:5 Rahab uses Hebrew
idiom; "I understand" (Josh. 2:9, Hebrew and LXX) becomes "knowing I know" (= "I certainly know"). Clement is providing local
color. His interpretation of the scarlet thread as prefigurative of the
Lord's blood recurs in Justin, *Dialogue* 111, 4, and in later authors.

It is interesting to observe that he provides no explicit quotations
from Leviticus or Numbers or the historical books of the Old Testament; these books provide historical examples for him and he either
alludes to them or paraphrases; see, especially, chapters 43 and 51
(also Judith and Esther in ch. 55).

13:1–19:1. This section begins with an exhortation to be "humble-
minded" (13:1)—the theme of the whole section and a subsidiary

tension and arrogance and foolishness and anger, and let us do
what is written. For the Holy Spirit says, "Let not the wise man
boast of his wisdom nor the strong man of his strength nor the
rich man of his wealth, but let him that boasts boast in the Lord,
so that he will seek him and do justice and righteousness" [Jer.
9:23, with vs. 24 adapted]. Above all, remember the words of
the Lord Jesus which he uttered while teaching forbearance and
patience, 2. "Be merciful, that you may receive mercy. Forgive,
that forgiveness may be given you; as you do, so it shall be done
to you; as you give, so shall it be given you; as you judge, so
shall you be judged; as you show kindness, so will kindness be
showed to you; the measure you give will be the measure you
get" [cf. Matt. 5:7; 6:14, 15; 7:1, 2, 12; Luke 6:31, 36–38]. 3. With
this commandment and these injunctions let us strengthen one
another for conduct obedient to his holy words in all humility;
for the holy Word says, 4. "On whom shall I look but on him

---

theme of other parts of the letter (see Kwa Joe Liang, *Het begrip
Demoed in 1 Clemens* [Utrecht, 1951]; also W. C. van Unnik in
Zeitschrift für die neutestamentliche Wissenschaft 44 [1952–53], 250–
255). In depicting this theme Clement uses two sets of expressions:
(1) those referring to the condition of humility—the verb *tapeinoun*
(18:7; 19:1; 59:3 twice), the noun *tapeinōsis* (16:7; 53:2; 55:6),
and the adjective *tapeinos* (30:2; 55:6; 59:3, 4); and (2) those referring to the attitude of humble-mindedness—the verb *tapeinophro-
noun* (2:1; 13:1, 3; 16:1, 2, 17; 17:2; 30:3; 48:6; 62:2), the noun
tapeinophrosyne (21:8; 30:8; 31:4; 44:3; 56:1; 58:2), and the adjective *tapeinophrōn* (19:1; 38:2). The latter set is by far the more
important (18/28 of the instances), and all the instances of the
former occur in biblical quotations or allusions or in passages based
on them. Clement's emphasis on humble-mindedness is characteristic
of Jewish piety and of the teaching of Jesus and of Paul (see Liang,
above; also Knopf p. 63), though he uses the two sets of words far
more often than do other Apostolic Fathers (Barnabas, nine times,
mostly in citations; Hermas, seven times, in relation to repentance and
fasting; Didache, once; Ignatius, once).
   The whole section is based (1) on quotations from the Old Testament and from the words of the Lord Jesus (13:1–15:6), and (2) on
the examples of Christ and of Old Testament heroes (16:1–19:1).
The quotations and examples are interspersed with brief sentences of
exhortation.
   13:1–4. The conclusion Clement draws from his examples (chs. 9–
12) is, as usual, the idea that Christians should be "humble-minded."
They should "do what is written" (cf. 43:1; 46:1–2; 53:1; also 1

that is humble and gentle and trembles at my words?" [Isa. 66:2.]

14 It is just and holy, therefore, brethren, that we should be obedient to God rather than follow those arrogant and unruly instigators of a detestable jealousy. 2. For we shall incur no insignificant harm but great danger if we recklessly give ourselves over to the purposes of those men who plunge into strife and dissension, to alienate us from the cause of right. 3. Let us show kindness to one another in accordance with the compassion and tenderness of him who created us. 4. For it is written, "The kind shall be the inhabitants of the land, and the innocent shall be left upon it; but those who transgress shall be destroyed from upon it" [Prov. 2:21–22; Ps. 36:9, 38]. 5. And again it says, "I

Cor. 4:6), for they are told what to do by the Holy Spirit (cf. 16:2–3). There follows a quotation from Jeremiah 9:23–24, in part identical with Paul's quotation in 1 Corinthians 1:31 (cf. 2 Cor. 10:17): "he who boasts must boast in (of) the Lord." Since the whole quotation does not come from Paul, it is doubtless derived from the text of Jeremiah, or an anthology containing the text, as commonly read among early Christians (see 15:1; 39:9).

In addition, Clement's readers are especially to remember the words of the Lord Jesus (the formula used in Acts 20:35) on forbearance and patience. The seven sayings have parallels in the Sermon on the Mount (Matt. 5–7; Luke 6), but as Koester (pp. 13–16) has indicated, Clement has not taken them directly from the Gospels. They are set forth in a stylized catechetical manner.

> (1–2) Do . . . so that you may be. . . .
> (3–4) As you . . . , thus it will be . . . to you.
> (5) As you . . . , thus you will be. . . .
> (6) As you . . . , thus it will be . . . to you.
> (7) With the measure you mete,
>   with it, it will be measured to you.

It cannot be determined whether this compilation was in circulation orally or in writing. Other sayings, following a quotation from "scripture," occur in 46:8.

Clement describes the sayings as a commandment, as ordinances, and as his (Jesus') hallowed words; he adds a further admonition given in "the holy Word" (cf. 56:3), from Isaiah 66:2.

14:1–5. Clement addresses his readers in a manner reminiscent of various Jewish speakers in Acts (ten times) as *andres adelphoi*, and his counsel also reminds one of Acts 5:29, where Peter says, "We must obey God rather than men." The men in question are charac-

saw the ungodly exalted and towering like the cedars of Lebanon; but I passed by and behold! he was no more, and I searched for his place and did not find it. Maintain innocence and righteousness, for a man of peace will have descendants" [Ps. 36:35–37].

15 Let us join ourselves, then, to those who are peaceable and godly and not to those who pretend to wish for it. 2. For it says in a certain passage, "This people honors me with their lips, but their heart is far from me" [Isa. 29:13; cf. Mark 7:6]. 3. And again, "They bless with their mouth, but curse with their heart" [Ps. 61:5]. 4. And again, "They loved him with their mouth, but with their tongue they lied to him, for their heart was not straightforward with him nor were they faithful to his covenant" [Ps. 77:36–37]. 5. Therefore, "let the deceitful tongues that speak lawlessness against the righteous be struck dumb" [Ps. 30:19]; and again, "May the Lord destroy all deceitful lips, the boastful tongue, those that say, 'We will praise [magnify?] our tongue, our lips are our own; who is Lord over us?' 6. Because of the wretchedness of the poor and the groans of the needy I will now arise, says the Lord; I will place him in safety. 7. I will act boldly in his cause" [Ps. 11:4–6].

---

terized by arrogance (see commentary on ch. 2) and anarchy (3:2; 43:6) and have promoted "detestable" (30:1) jealousy. Clement thus calls their morals as well as their obedience into question (cf. 47:5). He warns his readers against *recklessly* yielding to the ringleaders, who *plunge* into strife and sedition to *alienate* them from what is right. The words italicized are fairly unusual and occur in 1 Clement only here (except *alienate*, used of wives and husbands in 6:3); his sentence is rhetorical both in form and in content. His positive advice is to be kind to one another as the Creator is compassionate; this seems to reflect Ephesians 4:32: "Be kind to one another, compassionate, forgiving one another, as God in Christ has forgiven you." Be imitators of God; God's promises to the kind and peaceable are expressed in two Old Testament texts. The first is a combination of Proverbs 2:21 (according to Codex Sinaiticus and Codex Alexandrinus) and what looks like a mixture of Psalm 36:9 and Psalm 38 (closely parallel to Prov. 2:22). The second consists of Psalm 36:35–37. It is possible that Clement's attention was drawn to these verses by the beatitude about the lowly inheriting the earth (Matt. 5:5), for this is based on Psalm 36:11.

15:1–7.   The peacefulness of some is based on piety; that of others (the Corinthian leaders, cf. 14:1) is hypocritical. Christians should

16 For it is to the humble that Christ belongs, not to those
who exalt themselves over his flock. 2. The scepter of the majesty
of God, the Lord Jesus Christ, did not come with the pomp of
pride or arrogance, though he could have, but in humility, just
as the Holy Spirit said in speaking of him; 3. for it says, "Lord,
who has believed our report? Or to whom has the arm of the

---

join the former (see also 19:2; 30:3; 31:1; 46:4). Clement next provides Old Testament texts which show that hypocrisy in religion
exists and that God will condemn hypocrites. Each of the texts contains a mention of "lips" or "mouth" and in the first three there is a
contrast with "heart." The first text comes from Isaiah 29:13, but it
is quoted in a form closer to Mark 7:6 (cf. Matt. 15:8) than to the
Septuagint (cf. 39:9). The second is from Psalm 61:5; the third
from Psalm 77:36–37; the fourth from Psalm 30:19a–b; and the fifth
from Psalm 11:3–5.

In the Gospels, as in 2 Clement 3:5, the first quotation is ascribed
to or found in Isaiah, but here all the quotations are introduced with
"it says" or "again"; perhaps Clement is following an anthology and
either omitting references or not finding them.

Hatch (p. 205) wrongly supposed that independent evidence for
the existence of such an anthology was provided by Clement of
Alexandria; the later Clement is copying from the earlier one (*Str.*
4, 32, 2–33, 3). On the other hand, as we have argued in the introduction, the omission of fifteen words from the fourth and fifth texts
which Clement quotes may be due to his own carelessness in using
an anthology. The missing words are absent from every witness to
1 Clement except the Syriac version, and may have been restored by
an observant editor.

Meinhold (pp. 108–109) suggests that the quotations have a more
specific purpose: they are directed against the glossolalia which, in
his opinion, the Corinthians were practicing. He also compares the
descriptions of Moses (17:5–6) and David (18:12, 15), the emphasis
on "works, not words" (30:3; 38:2; cf. 21:5 and 2 Clem. 3 with
commentary) and the attack on the Corinthian leaders in 57:1–2
(Meinhold pp. 110–111). In all these instances it is possible that Clement has glossolalia in view; but his purpose may be more general.

16:1–17. Christ belongs to the humble-minded, not to those who
"lord it over" the sheepfold (1 Pet. 5:3) which is his, not theirs (for
"sheepfold" or "flock" as a term for the Church, see also Acts 20:28–
29; 1 Pet. 5:2; a favorite expression in Clement [cf. 44:3; 54:2; 57:2],
though he never mentions shepherds or, for that matter, except in
Old Testament quotations, sheep). Christ, though "the scepter of the
majesty of God" (an expression which sounds biblical but is not),
condescended—as in Philippians 2:6–8, where the verb *tapeinoun*
occurs—and was "humble-minded" (*tapeinophronōn*). In order to

Lord been revealed? We have made proclamation before him
that he is like a child, like a root in thirsty ground; he has no
comeliness nor glory. We saw him, and he had neither comeliness nor beauty, but his appearance was undistinguished, in-
ferior by human standards; a man of stripes and toil, knowing
what it is to endure weakness; for his face was turned away, he
was dishonored and disregarded. 4. He it is who bears our sins
and endures pain for us, while we considered him as one subject
to trouble and stripes and affliction. 5. But he was wounded for
our sins and suffered for our transgressions; the chastisement that
brought peace to us came upon him; by his stripes we were
healed. 6. Like sheep we have all gone astray, each one went
astray in his own way. 7. And the Lord gave him up for our
sins, but he did not open his mouth under mistreatment. Like a
sheep he was led away to be slaughtered, and as a lamb before
his shearers is dumb, so he did not open his mouth; in his humiliation justice was denied him. 8. Who will recount his posterity?
For his life was taken away from the earth. 9. Because of the
transgressions of my people he came to his death. 10. And I will
offer the wicked for his burial and the rich for his death, for he
did no iniquity, neither was deceit found in his mouth. And the
Lord wills to cleanse him of his stripes. 11. If you make an offering for your sin, your soul will see a long-lived posterity. 12. And
the Lord wills to remove his soul from toil, to show him light

---

prove this point Clement relies on what the Holy Spirit said in Isaiah
53:1–12 (53:7–8 is already quoted in Acts 8:32–33). Like Luke,
Clement reproduces the text of the Septuagint, in which the word
tapeinōsis is used to describe the situation (Isa. 53:8). In order to
complete the picture of Christ's humility he also quotes Psalm 21:7–9,
verses apparently already employed in various ways by the synoptic
evangelists in their descriptions of the crucifixion (Mark 15:29; Matt.
27:39; Luke 23:35).

Like Paul (2 Cor. 8:8–9; Phil. 2:3–8), Clement appeals to the
example of Christ's humiliation in order to encourage action on the
part of his correspondents. As elsewhere (5:7; 33:8), he uses the
word *hypogrammos* or "norm"—for the sake of variety from his more
usual *hypodeigma* (six times).

The expression "the yoke of his grace" is essentially Jewish; compare "the yoke of Torah" (*Mishna Aboth* 3, 8), the yoke of the kingdom of heaven (*Berakoth* 13a, noted by C. Taylor, *Sayings of the
Jewish Fathers*, 2d. ed. [Cambridge, 1897], 46), the yoke of Wisdom
(Sir. 51:26), and the yoke of Jesus (Matt. 11:29–30).

and inform him with understanding, to justify a righteous man who serves many well; for he himself will bear their sins. 13. Therefore he shall have many heirs and a share in the spoils of the strong, because for them his life was given up to death and he was numbered among the transgressors. 14. For he it was who bore the sins of many and because of their sins was delivered up" [Isa. 53]. 15. And again he himself says, "I am a worm and not a man, a disgrace to mankind and despised by the people. 16. All who see me mocked me, they spoke with their mouths, they shook their heads—'He hoped in the Lord, let him deliver him; let him save him, since he desires him'" [Ps. 21:7–9]. 17. You see, beloved brethren, what an example has been given us! For if the Lord himself was so humble, what should we do who have come under the yoke of his grace?

17 Let us become imitators of such as went about "in the skins of goats and sheep" [Heb. 11:37], preaching the coming of Christ; we mean Elijah and Elisha, and Ezekiel too, the prophets, and the meritorious figures of old as well. 2. Abraham's merit was gloriously attested and he was called the friend of God, yet when he beheld the glory of God he said humbly, "I am but

---

17:1–6. For prophetic anticipation of Christ's coming, see especially 1 Peter 1:10–12; for imitation of the heroes of faith, Hebrews 6:12; and for the description of the prophets as wearing skins of goats and sheep, Hebrews 11:37. From the Old Testament (3 Regn. [= 1 Kings] 19:13, 19; 4 Regn. [= 2 Kings] 2) Clement knows that Elijah and Elisha wore such garb; from Zechariah 13:4 (LXX) he knows that it is characteristic of all prophets, and that thus they expressed their humility.

In setting forth the examples which follow, Clement follows a fixed form. First he indicates why the hero can be regarded as approved by God; then he supplies evidence of the hero's humility. (1) Abraham was called "friend of God" (10:1; Jas. 2:23), but when he beheld God's glory (cf. John 12:41, of Isaiah) he called himself "dust and ashes" (Gen. 18:27). (2) Scripture tells us that Job was absolutely righteous (Job 1:1), but he himself said that no one is pure from defilement (Job 14:4–5). (3) Moses was called "faithful in all God's house" (Num. 12:7; cf. Heb. 3:2, 5); God judged Egypt through him; he was given great glory (cf. Heb. 3:3); but when he received an oracle (cf. 55:1; Rom. 11:4; Ziegler pp. 64–65) "out of the bush" (Exod. 3:2–4), he made the statements found in Exodus 3:11 and 4:10. In addition, he expressed his humility in a saying probably from

dust and ashes" [Gen. 18:27]. 3. Once again, of Job it is written, "Job was righteous and blameless, sincere, devout, keeping himself from any form of evil" [Job 1:1]. 4. Yet he accuses himself in these words, "There is none who is free from stain, should his life span be but a single day" [Job 14:4–5]. 5. Then there is Moses, who is called "faithful in all God's house" [Num. 12:7; Heb. 3:2, 5], through whose service God brought judgment upon Egypt with afflictions and torments; but though he was so greatly glorified, he did not boast, but when the oracle was given him from the bush he said, "Who am I that thou shouldst send me? For I have a weak voice and am slow of speech" [Exod. 3:11; 4:10]. 6. And again he [it?] says, "I am but vapor from a pot" [source unknown].

18 And what are we to say of the famous David, to whom God said, "I have found a man after my own heart, David the son of Jesse; I have anointed him with eternal mercy" [1 Regn. (=1 Sam.) 13:14; Ps. 88:21; cf. Acts 13:22]. 2. But he himself says to God, "Have mercy upon me, O God, according to thy great

---

some apocryphal document (cf. J. R. Harris in *Journal of Biblical Literature* 29 [1910], 190–195).

The text from Job is quoted by the Gnostic Basilides (Clement, *Str.* 4, 83) as proving the universality of sin; see also Origen as quoted by K. Aland, *Did the Early Church Baptize Infants?* (Philadelphia, 1963), 47, n. 1. This is clearly not, however, what Clement has in mind.

18:1–17. As we have just seen (17:1–2), Clement likes to refer to Old Testament heroes as "well attested" or "approved" or "famous" (cf. Heb. 11:2, 4–5, 39; also 1 Clem. 19:1, conclusion of this section; 44:3, presbyters; 47:4, apostles). The famous David was approved by God, according to Psalm 88:21 and 1 Samuel 13:14 (run together as in Acts 13:22). Clement is not quoting from Acts (E. Haenchen, *Die Apostelgeschichte* [Göttingen, 1957], 1–2) but may be using an anthology also reflected in Acts (cf. L. Cerfaux in *Aux souces de la tradition chrétienne (Mélanges Goguel)* [Neuchatel, 1950], 43–51). Though approved by God, David himself expressed his humility in Psalm 50:3–19, quoted almost exactly from the Septuagint. Knopf (p. 72) points out that the psalm does not deal specifically or simply with humility; but conceivably Clement took it from an anthology. **19:1.** Clement now sums up the point he has been making since the beginning of chapter 13. The humility of the heroes he has mentioned ("so many and such celebrated," as in a later sum-

mercy, and according to the abundance of thy pity blot out my transgression. 3. Wash me thoroughly from my iniquity, and cleanse me from my sin; for I acknowledge my iniquity and my sin is ever before me. 4. Against thee only have I sinned and done that which is evil in thy sight, that thou mayest be justified in thy words and prevail when thou art judged. 5. For behold, I was brought forth in iniquity and in sin did my mother conceive me. 6. For behold, thou lovest truth; the secret and hidden things of thy wisdom thou makest known to me. 7. Sprinkle me with hyssop, and I shall be clean; wash me and I shall be whiter than snow. 8. Thou shalt make me hear of joy and gladness, the bones that have been humbled will rejoice. 9. Turn away thy face from my sins, and blot out all my iniquity. 10. Create a clean heart in me, O God, and renew a right spirit within me. 11. Drive me not away from thy presence, and take not thy holy spirit from me. 12. Restore to me the joy of thy salvation and strengthen me with thy guiding spirit. 13. I shall teach transgressors thy way, and the godless shall turn to thee. 14. Deliver me from bloodguiltiness, O God, the God of my salvation. 15. My tongue shall rejoice in thy righteousness. O Lord, open thou my mouth and my lips will proclaim thy praise. 16. For if thou didst desire sacrifice, I would give it thee; but in burnt offerings thou art not pleased. 17. The sacrifice of God is a broken spirit; a broken and contrite heart, O God, thou wilt not despise" [Ps. 50:3–19].

19 The humility and obedient submission of so many and such celebrated men have improved not only us but also the generations before us, all who have received his oracles in fear and in truth.

E. God's providential order and its peace (19:2–20:12)

2. Since then we share in many great and glorious deeds, let

mary, 63:1) has improved us and, as well, earlier generations (in old and new Israel alike) who have received God's oracles (the Old Testament; cf. 13:4; 53:1; 62:3).

19:2–20:12. After a brief summary of the preceding section on humility and obedience (19:1), Clement announces the next section, which will deal with peace as revealed and given by "the Father and

us hasten toward the goal of peace that was originally given us, and let us fix our eyes on the Father and Creator of the universe and cling to his splendid and superlative gift and benefit of peace. 3. Let us contemplate him with understanding and perceive with the eyes of the soul his patient purpose; let us consider how free from anger he is toward all his creation.

20 The heavens move at his direction and peacefully obey him. 2. Day and night complete the course appointed by him, nor in-

---

Creator of the universe." He also points toward the section after that when he speaks of God's "patient purpose" and his lack of wrath; man owes a response to God, in order to escape his wrath (chs. 21–39). First, however, Clement urges his readers to contemplate God with their understanding—equivalent to "the eyes of the soul" (19:3). As Bardy, Jaeger, and others have argued, Clement is clearly following a Stoic source, as he describes the harmony and peace of the cosmos in chapter 20, though he makes it his own largely by introducing language based on the Septuagint.

19:2–3.   Clement now imitates a transitional sentence from Hebrews (12:1) which speaks of "such a cloud of witnesses" and of running the race set before us. He refers to the goal of peace as handed down to us from the beginning (of creation, as the following passage shows) and urges his readers (1) to look toward "the Father and Creator of the universe" and (2) to cling to his gifts of peace and to his benefits (his beneficent gifts of peace). Such an idea is clearly Hellenistic (examples in Knopf p. 75); it is also characteristic of Hellenistic Judaism. The way to look toward God is to use our understanding, equivalent to "the eyes of the soul" ("eyes of the heart," 59:3; "understanding" and "eyes of the heart," 36:2; also Eph. 1:18); compare K. E. Kirk, *The Vision of God* (London, 1932). If we consider his long-suffering will, we can consider how free of wrath he is toward his creation in spite of its disobedience.

20:1–12.   According to Knopf (p. 76; after Drews), this chapter is "a piece of old Roman liturgy, though naturally preserved in free use." Such an analysis is not justified either by parallels such as Theophilus, *Ad Autol.* 1, 6–7, or by echoes of Clement in later liturgies. The chapter reflects Clement's concern for cosmic order and was constructed by him (like the prayer in chs. 59–61) in relation to dissent at Corinth. Nothing whatever is known of the Roman liturgy, if there was one, in Clement's time. Clement's point is that peaceful providential order, established throughout the universe by God, exists for the benefit of mankind. The point is essentially Stoic in origin, although as W. C. van Unnik has shown (*Vigiliae Christianae* 4 [1950], 181–189), there are Jewish parallels, Hellen-

terfere with one another. 3. Sun and moon and the chorus of
stars travel on their appointed courses according to his ordi-
nance, in harmony and with never a deviation. 4. By his will the
earth becomes fruitful at the appointed seasons, yielding food in
abundance for man and beast, neither dissenting nor altering
anything decreed by him. 5. The inscrutable and indescribable
judgments of the abyss and the underworld are held together by
the same decrees. 6. The basin of the boundless sea being firmly
fixed by his creative action for their gathering together, the
waters do not overpass the bounds thus set but do as he commanded them. 7. For he said, "Thus far shall you come, and
your waves shall break within you" [Job 38:11]. 8. The ocean
which men cannot pass and the worlds beyond it are governed

---

istic and apocalyptic. The most significant parallels occur in Cicero,
De natura deorum 2, 98–127 (from Greek Stoic sources); see also
Sanders pp. 109–130. Clement, or a predecessor, has combined these
ideas with biblical phrases (cf. 33:3–4).

Clement begins with the heavens, day and night (cf. 24:3), sun,
moon, and stars. Here his theme, like some of his language, is clearly
related to the Psalms (Knopf)—especially Psalm 18(19):1–2 (cited
27:7): "The heavens declare the glory of God. . . . One day telleth
another; and one night certifieth another" (BCP). But the same
themes, in the same order, are expressed in such contemporary literature as the *Placita* of Aetius (Sanders pp. 112–113), the pseudo-
Aristotelian treatise *De mundo* (*ibid.*, pp. 115–118), and the twelfth
Oration of Dio Chrysostom (*ibid.*, pp. 121–122).

Next comes the earth, viewed as a living being (Mother Earth, as
Jaeger observed) as by Greek writers; on the other hand, Clement's
use of "abyss" recalls the Old Testament ("abyss" in Job 38:16, a
passage to which he is turning), while the "basin" of the sea recalls
Psalm 64:8 (Sinaiticus), and "gathering together" is from Genesis
1:9. The "bounds" placed around the sea are from Job 38:10, and
Clement quotes the next verse in Job immediately.

The themes which follow are Greek. The Atlantic Ocean (cf. 5:7)
is so large that it cannot be crossed, though there are "worlds"
(Atlantis? India?) beyond it (for these themes see Strabo, *Geog.* 1,
1, 8; 1, 4, 6; 2, 3, 6; Lightfoot pp. 72–73; Knopf pp. 80–81); but
God controls it and them. The changing seasons (known through
[Greek] wisdom, Wisd. 7:18) are equally regular—as Stoic writers
were aware. The various orders of the winds (cf. Job. 28:25) also
accomplish "their service"; this is a Jewish-Christian term, but the
idea is expressed by Graeco-Roman writers.

Clement terminates his discussion by speaking of springs (Cicero,
De natura deorum 2, 120–122) and the unions of the smallest animals

by the same decrees of the Master. 9. The seasons of spring, summer, autumn, and winter peacefully give way to one another. 10. The winds from their quarters perform their service without disturbance, each at its proper time. Perennial springs, created for enjoyment and health, unfailingly offer their life-giving breasts to men. The smallest animals accomplish their mating in harmony and peace. 11. All these things the great Creator and Master of the universe ordered to exist in peace and harmony, so lavishing his goodness upon everyone and most abundantly upon us who have taken refuge in his mercy through our Lord Jesus Christ, 12. to whom be glory and majesty forever and ever. Amen.

F. Man's moral response to God (21:1–22:8)

21 Beware, beloved, lest his many benefits turn out to be our condemnation, as will happen if we do not conduct ourselves

---

(*ibid.*, 123). According to W. Jaeger (*Rheinisches Museum* 102 [1959], 335–340), the mention of the breasts of the springs, with the poetic word *mazoi*, is based on an unidentifiable verse from a tragic poet. It is quite possible, however, that Clement either substituted *mazoi* for the more common *mastoi* found in such a parallel as Philo, *De opificio mundi* 133, or derived it from a philosophical source already tinged with poetic language. As for the smallest animals, J. J. Thierry has shown (*Vigiliae Christianae* 14 [1960], 235–244) that "mating" refers to sexual union.

The summary reiterates the theme of cosmic concord, ascribing it to the Demiurge and Master of the universe, who gives benefits to all and especially to Christians, who have "taken refuge in his mercy" (a phrase that recalls biblical language but does not occur in the Bible) through our Lord Jesus Christ. A doxology concludes this section, as in 32:4; 38:4; 43:6; 45:7; 50:7; 58:2; 61:3; ch. 64; 65:2. The doxologies emphasize the solemnity of what has been said and often precede exhortations. They do not mark divisions within the letter.

21:1–22:8. The benefits which God has conferred upon his creation require men to respond to him by living in harmony. God knows men's thoughts and therefore Christians must strive to recover the lost radiance of the original Corinthian situation (1:2–2:8). Proof that God actually desires this response and rewards it is then provided from the Psalms.

21:1–9. Christians must live in a way worthy of God, that is, in the harmony described as cosmic in chapter 20, for otherwise he, who

worthily of him and accomplish in harmony that which is excellent and well pleasing in his sight. 2. For as it says somewhere, "The Spirit of the Lord is a lamp searching out the hidden chambers of the heart" [Prov. 20:27 paraphrased]. 3. Let us realize how near he is, and that none of our thoughts nor any of the rationalizations in which we indulge escape him. 4. Hence it is right that we should not desert from his will. 5. Far better to offend foolish and thoughtless men who exalt themselves and take pride in their pretentious utterance than to offend God. 6. Let us revere the Lord Jesus Christ whose blood was given for us; let us respect our rulers, honor our elders, train our youth in the discipline of the fear of God, guide our women toward what is good. 7. Let them exemplify that purity of character that deserves to be loved, [let them] display a sincere and gentle disposition, and by their silence make evident the restraint of their tongues; let them hold in equal affection, without favoritism, all those who fear God. 8. Let us have our children participate in Christian nurture that they may learn what humility avails with God, what power pure love has with him, how good and great is the fear of him and that it saves all who

---

knows men's thoughts, will punish them. Men who belong to his army must not desert (cf. 28:2; 37:2–3; Ignatius, Polyc. 6:2). It is better to offend the schismatics than God (so 14:1).

The way in which to obey God is now set forth in a recapitulation of earlier passages.

blood of the Lord Jesus Christ	7:4
rulers-presbyters (older men)	1:3
young-wives	1:3

The virtues enjoined upon them are closely similar to those mentioned before (1:3). When children share in "Christian nurture" (cf. Jaeger pp. 24–26), they learn

what strength humility has before God (cf. Phil. 4:13)
what power pure love has before God (cf. 1 Cor. 13:4–7; 1 Clem. 49)
how fear of him is good and great, and saves

Knopf p. 84 quotes the relevant Greek Old Testament passages about God's breath (Gen. 2:7; Prov. 24:12; Ps. 103:29; and Job 34:14–15) but wrongly says that Stoic parallels (are they parallel?) should be considered too. Clement's thought is closer to biblical anthropomorphism (see commentary on 28:2 and 33:4; cf. Theophilus, Ad Autol. 1, 7).

live in it with holiness and a pure mind. 9. For he is the searcher
of thoughts and of desires [cf. Heb. 4:12]; whose breath animates
us and when he wills to do so he will take it away.

22 Now Christian faith confirms all this; for Christ himself
summons us thus through the Holy Spirit:
"Come, children, listen to me
I will teach you the fear of the Lord.
2. What man is there that desires life
and loves to see good days?
3. Keep your tongue from evil
and your lips from speaking deceit.
4. Depart from evil and do good:
5. seek peace, and pursue it.
6. The eyes of the Lord are toward the righteous
and his ears toward their cry,
but the face of the Lord is against evildoers,
to cut off the remembrance of them from the earth.
7. When the righteous man cried for help,
the Lord heard him, and delivered him out of all his
troubles [Ps. 33:12–18].

22:1–8. Just as in 16:2 Clement ascribes the words of Isaiah 53
to the Holy Spirit, so here he ascribes verses from the Psalms to
Christ speaking through the Holy Spirit (cf. 63:2). These verses confirm the teaching of chapter 21 ("all these things"). The quotation
which Clement gives is composite; it consists of Psalm 33:12–18 and
Psalm 31:10 (cf. Hatch p. 205). The way in which he continues
after the quotations (33:1) suggests that something has gone wrong
with the text, for he is emphasizing God's goodness, not his punishment of sinners.

At the end of his quotation from Psalm 33 Clement reads, "The
righteous man cried for help; the Lord heard him and delivered him
out of all his troubles." This is practically identical with Psalm 33:18;
verse 19 reads, "The Lord is near to those whose heart is humbled,
and he will save the lowly [*tapeinous*] of spirit." Why did Clement
not quote this? It conveys his message exactly—and in the Syriac
version of his letter Psalm 33:20 has been inserted (but not vs. 19).
Instead, he turns to Psalm 31:10, which admittedly contrasts God's
mercy on those who set their hope on him with his punishment of the
sinner, but is not so appropriate for his purpose. Presumably he was
using an anthology, not the text of the Psalms. The strangely com-

8. Many are the pangs of the sinner,
>   but mercy will surround him who hopes in the Lord" [Ps. 31:10].

G. The eschatological sanction (23:1–28:4)

23 The all-merciful and beneficent Father has mercy upon those who fear him, and kindly and lovingly bestows his favor upon those who approach him in singleness of mind. 2. Wherefore let us not be double-minded, neither let our souls entertain false ideas about his surpassing and glorious gifts. 3. Far be that Scripture from us which says, "Wretched are the double-minded, those who harbor doubts in their souls and say, 'We have heard these things even in our fathers' time, and yet here we are, already grown old, and none of these things has happened to us.' 4. O senseless ones! Compare yourselves to a tree. Take a vine, for instance: first it sheds its leaves, then comes a bud, then a leaf, then a flower, and only after this, first a green grape and

---

posite character of other psalm quotations points toward this conclusion.

23:1–28:4. The following six chapters are devoted to the eschatological sanction for the virtues which in God's name Clement has demanded of the Corinthians. He begins with a transitional chapter attacking doubts about the Lord's coming (cf. 2 Pet. 3:4) and then proceeds to show that God has provided analogical proofs of the future resurrection, as well as explicit testimonies in scripture (chs. 24–26); moreover, God is omnipotent and omnipresent (chs. 27–28).

23:1–4. At the beginning of this chapter, as Knopf p. 85 points out, Clement picks up themes which he has been treating just previously; most of the words have occurred in chapters 19–22. He mentions "singleness of mind" (only here in the letter) because he is about to quote "the Scripture" against the "double-minded" (doubters; cf. the example of Lot's wife, 11:2) whose fancies run away with them. This scripture is also quoted, as "the prophetic word," in 2 Clement 11:2–4. We supply a very literal translation.

1 Clement	*2 Clement*
Wretched are the double-minded	Wretched are the double-minded
who doubt in [their] *soul*	who doubt in [their] *heart*
and say, These things we heard	and say, These things we heard
even in the time	*long ago and* in the time
of our fathers, *and behold,*	of our fathers, *but waiting from*

then a ripe one." You see how in a short space of time the fruit of the tree reaches maturity. 5. Truly his purpose will be quickly and suddenly accomplished, just as the Scripture confirms when it says, "He will come quickly and not delay, and the Lord will come suddenly to his temple, even the Holy One whom you expect" [Isa. 13:22 LXX; Mal. 3:1].

---

we have grown old, and none of them *has happened to us.*	*day to day we have seen* none of them.
O foolish men, compare yourselves	Foolish men, compare yourselves
with a tree; take a vine;	with a tree; take a vine;
first it sheds its leaves,	first it sheds its leaves,
then there comes a bud,	then there comes a bud,
then a leaf, then a flower,	
and after these an unripe grape	after these an unripe grape,
then the full bunch.	then the full bunch.
	So also my people has had tumults and
	afflictions; then it will receive good things.

The parallel would be even closer were we to read "bud-leaf-flower" in 2 Clement—as seems to be implied by "after these things." The quotation, obviously from a Jewish apocryphal writing (E. Nestle in *Zeitschrift für die neutestamentliche Wissenchaft* 1 [1900], 180), is not taken from 1 Clement in 2 Clement; both documents are directly based on it. In both documents it is combined with an injunction not to be double-minded (1 Clem. 23:2; 2 Clem. 11:5).

23:5. Clement continues with the statement that Scripture also (hence from the same document?) testifies that God's will—that is, his eschatological purpose—will be accomplished "quickly" and "suddenly"; both words occur in the mixed quotation which he provides, partly from Isaiah 13:22 (with present tense of LXX changed to future; cf. Hab. 2:3), partly from Malachi 3:1. In the latter verse there are considerable changes.

Malachi 3:1 (LXX)	*Clement*
The Lord, whom you seek,	The Lord
will suddenly come to his temple,	will suddenly come to his temple,
and the Messenger of the Covenant,	even the Holy One,
whom you desire.	whom you expect.

"The Holy One" is a title of Christ in Revelation 3:7 and probably in 1 John 2:20 (R. Bultmann, *Das Evangelium des Johannes* [Göttingen, 1941], 344, n. 5); see also Acts 3:14. A different Greek word (*hosios*) with a similar meaning ("thy Holy One") occurs in

24 Let us consider, beloved, how the Master continually points out that future resurrection which is to be, of which he made our Lord Jesus Christ the first fruits when he raised him from the dead. 2. Let us observe, beloved, the resurrection that occurs in the regularity of the seasons. 3. Day and night manifest resurrection: night falls asleep, and day arises; day departs, night returns. 4. Or take for example the crops: how and in what way is the sowing done? 5. The sower goes out and sows each seed in the ground, and they fall to the earth dry and bare, and decay. Then from their decay the wondrous providence of the Master raises them, and from each one more grow and bear fruit.

25 Let us take note of the remarkable and symbolic phenomenon encountered in the East, that is, in the vicinity of Arabia.

Psalm 15 (16):10 and is applied to Christ in Acts 2:27. And the title "the Holy One of God" is clearly Messianic in Mark 1:24 (Luke 4:34) and John 6:69. For the phrase "whom you expect" see Matthew 11:3 and Luke 7:19–20. Clement's quotation is thus clearly Messianic, whether Jewish or Christian.

24:1–5.   Clement now urges his readers to "consider" (34:5; 37:2; cf. 47:5) the proof which the Master provides for a future resurrection. The statement that he made Christ its "first fruits" (1 Cor. 15:20) by raising from the dead does not seem to be a part of the proof, since Clement repeats his injunction to "consider" in the word "let us observe." What we observe is seasonal resurrection in the realm of nature—though for Clement the order of nature is not self-sufficient but the consequence of creation (20:11; chs. 27, 33). The "proofs" which Clement gives come from Stoic selections of analogies which demonstrate the existence of cosmic (not individual) renewal. These are as follows: (1) day and night (Seneca, *Ep.* 36, 11); (2) seeds (*Stoicorum veterum fragmenta* II, 596, 618). Clement Christianizes his sources by making an allusion to the parable of the sower (Matt. 13:3 ff.; Mark 4:3 ff.; Luke 8:5 ff.; Gospel of Thomas, p. 82, n. 3) along with a paraphrase of Paul's discussion of the seed in 1 Corinthians 15:36 and perhaps 2 Corinthians 5:3. The seed's bringing forth fruit is derived either from the synoptic parable or from John 12:24. The emphasis on "the wondrous providence of the Master" is Clement's own—or in part that of his Stoic source or informants.

On the use of Stoic materials by Christian apologists for resurrection, see R. M. Grant, *Miracle and Natural Law in Graeco-Roman and Early Christian Thought* (Amsterdam, 1952), 235–245.

25:1–5.   Proof of the resurrection is provided not only by natural

2. For there is a bird which is called the phoenix. It is the only one of its kind and lives five hundred years. When the hour of its death approaches, it makes itself a nest out of frankincense and myrrh and other spices, and when its time has come it gets into it and dies. 3. Then as its flesh decays a kind of worm is produced which is nourished by the secretions of the carcass and grows wings. Then when it is grown it takes the nest containing the bones of its predecessor and manages to carry them all the way from Arabia to the Egyptian city called Heliopolis. 4. Whereupon in broad daylight, in plain sight of everyone, it alights upon the altar of the sun and deposits them there; and

---

natural phenomena but also by an unnatural natural phenomenon: the phoenix. The story of the phoenix produced a good deal of doubt among later Christian writers, even those who knew Clement's letter, though Tertullian, Lactantius, Cyril of Jerusalem, and a few others were willing to accept it as true—as Clement himself was (cf. J. Hubaux and M. Leroy, *Le mythe du phénix dans les littératures grecque et latine* [Liège-Paris, 1939], 189). Parallels are provided by Lightfoot pp. 84–89 and Knopf pp. 88–89, but they can be considerably simplified if with Sanders pp. 72–73 we observe that nearly all the details in Clement's version correspond with the accounts in Pomponius Mela (*Chorogr.* 3, 8; A.D. 40/41) and Pliny the Elder (*Nat. hist.* 10, 4; before A.D. 79). This is to say that Clement's version is essentially Roman in origin. These details can be summarized as follows:

from Arabia	Pliny
a unique specimen	Pomponius Mela
lives 500 years	Aelian, *Nat. animal.* 6, 58
coffin of . . . myrrh and other aromas	Pomponius Mela Pliny
decomposes	Manilius in Pliny, *Nat. hist.* 10, 4
worm emerges	Pliny
grows wings	*fieri pullum*, Pliny
to Egypt—Heliopolis	Pomponius Mela, Pliny
by day in the sight of all	Johannes Lydus, *De mensibus* 4, 11
altar of the sun	Pomponius Mela, Pliny
priests check records	Aelian, *Nat. animal.* 6, 58

The basic account is thus close to Pomponius Mela and Pliny, though various details are paralleled only in later Greek writers, who presumably use earlier sources (Lydus says he is using Apollonius, probably of Tyana, 4, 11).

Clement probably takes his "paradoxical sign" from some writer who deals with marvels (cf. Grant, *Miracle and Natural Law*, 94, also 210 and index 278 *s.v.* Animals, Phoenix).

then starts back again. 5. The priests then consult their record of dates and find that it has come at the end of the five-hundredth year.

26 Are we to think it then a great and wondrous thing if the Creator of all things causes to be raised from the dead those who have served him in holiness and in the assurance of a good faith, when even in the case of a bird he shows us the greatness of his promise? 2. For it says somewhere, "And thou shalt raise me up and I shall praise thee" [Ps. 27:7 paraphrased], and "I lay down and slept: I rose up again [Ps. 3:6], because thou art with me" [Ps. 22:4]. 3. And again Job says, "And thou shalt raise up this flesh of mine which has endured all these things" [Job 19:26 paraphrased].

27 Having this hope, then, let our souls be bound to him who is faithful to his promises and just in his judgments. 2. He it is

---

26:1–3. "Great and wondrous" is an expression which Clement likes (50:1; 53:3 [from Deut. 9:14]); compare "blessed and wonderful" (35:1). For "any wonder" in a question see 43:1; in this usage it introduces an argument *a minore ad maius*, with which Knopf p. 90 compares Tertullian's similar statement in *De resurrectione carnis* 13, 4. The Creator of the universe can raise those who served him in holiness and in faith, when he has already raised the phoenix. For the phrase "in the assurance of a good faith" see Ephesians 3:12 and Titus 2:10 (also 1 Clem. 35:2; Lightfoot p. 89).

After all, the Old Testament itself clearly speaks of resurrection—or so Clement believes, following either his memory or an earlier anthology. The quotations are not very exact.

And thou shalt raise me up, and I shall praise thee, and I lay down and slept: I rose up again, because thou art with me.	Ps. 27:7 and my flesh flowered again, and . . . I will praise thee.
	Ps. 3:6 I lay down and slept, I was raised
	Ps. 22:4 for thou art with me.
(And again Job says,) And thou shalt raise up this flesh of mine which has endured all these things.	Job 19:26 (Codex Alexandrinus) he will raise my body which endures these things.

27:1–7. Our souls can be bound, because of this hope, to God who promises faithfully (Heb. 10:23; 11:11) and judges justly (a common biblical theme). He has commanded men not to lie (e.g., in the Decalogue); his omnipotence (another biblical theme) is limited

who commanded us not to lie: how much the more will he not lie himself! For the one thing that is impossible to God is to be false. 3. Let our faith in him then be rekindled in us, and bear in mind that all things are near him. 4. By the word of his majesty he established all things, and by his word he can bring them to nought. 5. "Who will say to him, 'What have you done?' Or who can stand against the might of his power?" [Wisd. 12:12; 11:22]. When he wills and as he wills he shall accomplish all things, and not one of the things he has decreed can fail. 6. All things lie open to his sight, and nothing has escaped his will, 7. since "the heavens are telling the glory of God, and the firmament proclaims his handiwork; day to day pours forth speech and night to night declares knowledge; yet there are neither words nor speech, and their voices are not heard" [Ps. 18:2-4].

28 Since then all things are seen and heard [by him], let us fear him and desist from base actions spawned by wanton desires. 2. For where can any of us flee from his mighty hand? What world is there to receive one who deserts from him? 3. For the Scripture somewhere says, "Where shall I go and where

---

only by his inability to lie (cf. Heb. 6:18). Our faith in him can be "rekindled" (cf. 2 Tim. 1:6; Ignatius, Eph. 1:1) on this ground, and we must recognize that everything is near him, that is, he is close enough to know men's thoughts and to judge them (21:3, 9; Eggenberger p. 169 misunderstands the expression). He made all things by his word (Word? cf. Heb. 1:3) and by his word he can destroy them (21:9). A tacit quotation from Wisdom 12:12 and 11:22 confirms the doctrine of God's omnipotence. He is also omnipresent. Heaven and earth declare God's glory and his creative power, as is shown in Psalm 18(19):1-3.

Eggenberger p. 169 claims that chapter 27 is intended to weaken the eschatological notes in chapters 28-29; it is hard to see how this could be so.

28:1-4. Since God is all-seeing and all-hearing (cf. Homer, *Od.* 11, 108; Josephus, *Ant.* 8, 108; Theophilus, *Ad Autol.* 2, 3; 37), we must fear him and abandon (even) our desires for wicked deeds; there are judgments to come (note the eschatological emphasis, as in chs. 22-24; 26-27). Since he is "near" (21:3, cf. 27:3), there is no place of refuge from him, and no "world" that can receive deserters (21:4; Ignatius, Polyc. 6:2); for the "worlds" even beyond the ocean are ruled by God (20:8). This point is confirmed by a very inexact quotation from "the writing" (*grapheion*, perhaps indicating a division

shall I hide from thy face? If I go up into heaven, thou art there;
if I go off to the ends of the earth, there is thy right hand; if I
make my bed in the abyss, there is thy Spirit" [Ps. 138:7–9
paraphrased]. 4. Where then can one go to escape from him
who embraces all things?

H. Holiness and its duties (29:1–30:8)

29 Let us then approach him in holiness of life, lifting up to
him pure and undefiled hands, with love for our gentle and
compassionate Father who has made us a chosen portion for

---

of the Old Testament as *grapheia* does in Epiphanius' description of
Jewish Christian views: "the law and the prophets and the writings,"
Pan. 29, 7, 2. 4).

Clement	*Psalm 138:7–9*
Where shall I go and	Where shall I go from thy Spirit, and
where shall I hide from thy face?	where shall I flee from thy face?
If I go up into heaven, thou art there;	If I go up into heaven, thou art there;
if I go off to the ends of the earth, there is thy right hand;	if I go down into Hades, thou art present;
if I make my bed in the abyss, there is thy Spirit.	if I take my wings outspread and tabernacle at the ends of the sea,
	even there thy hand will lead me,
	and thy right hand will hold me.

Indeed, the Septuagint quotation leads up more naturally to Clement's conclusion: a man cannot depart or escape from God, who "embraces all things." For this notion Knopf p. 93 provides Stoic parallels,
but it is probable (in view of the mention of "hands" in 29:1) that
Clement's thought is more anthropomorphic (cf. Theophilus, *Ad
Autol.* 1, 5).

29:1–30:8.   These two chapters are concerned with holiness and
its duties; first Clement shows that Christians are the portion of the
one who is holy (ch. 29) and then he indicates the ethical implica-
tions of holiness. Both chapters are based on anthologies of Old
Testament quotations.

29:1–3.   If one cannot escape from God (ch. 28), one should with
holiness of soul (cf. "purity of heart," 32:4 and commentary) approach him, raising pure and undefiled hands to him in the ancient
attitude of prayer (cf. Knopf p. 93; closer parallels in Lightfoot p.

himself. 2. For thus it is written, "When the Most High divided the nations, when he scattered the descendants of Adam, he set the boundaries of the nations according to the number of the angels of God. But the portion of the Lord was his people Jacob, Israel was his allotment" [Deut. 32:8–9]. 3. And in another place it says, "Behold, the Lord is taking for himself a people from the midst of the nations [Deut. 4:34] as a man takes the first fruits of his threshing floor, and out of that people shall come the holiest offerings."

30 Since then we are a holy portion, let us accomplish all that pertains to holiness; fleeing from slander, vile and impure embraces, drunkenness and rebellion and filthy lusts, detestable adultery and foul arrogance. 2. "For God," it says, "resists the arrogant but gives grace to the humble" [Prov. 3:34; cf. Jas. 4:6; 1 Pet. 5:5]. 3. So let us join those to whom grace is given by God. Let us clothe ourselves with harmony in humility and self-control, keeping ourselves far from gossip and slander, being justified in deed and not in word. 4. For it says, "He who speaks much will hear much in reply; or does the babbler imagine he is right? 5. Blessed is he born of woman who is short-lived. Be not profuse in speech" [Job 11:2–3]. 6. Let our praise be of God and not from ourselves; for God hates those who praise them-

---

93: 1 Tim. 2:8; Athenagoras, *Leg.* 13). God has elected both the old Israel and the new (cf. 1 Pet. 2:9) or, it would be better to say, there is only one Israel, culminating in the "flock of Christ."

The quotation from Deuteronomy 32:8–9 shows that for Clement the Church is the true successor of "Jacob" and "Israel" in the Old Testament. His second quotation proves the same point; it begins with Deuteronomy 4:34 (freely quoted) but continues with verses which sound like the Old Testament but do not come from it. He may be remembering such verses as Deuteronomy 14:2, Numbers 18:27, 2 Chronicles 31:14, and Ezekiel 48:12; or he may be using something like the apocryphal Ezekiel (cf. commentary on ch. 8).

30:1–8. From (the new) Israel's election Clement infers that Christians are bound to express their holiness in deeds of holiness. They are to flee from seven vices mostly sexual in nature—but in the middle of the list comes "rebellion"; Clement always keeps his main purpose in mind. The same point is clear from the fact that he ends with pride so that he can quote Proverbs 3:34 on the proud and the humble (also in Jas. 4:6; 1 Pet. 5:5). Since God favors the humble,

selves. 7. Let the testimony to our good conduct be given by
others, as it was given in the case of our forefathers who were
righteous. 8. Arrogance and self-will and recklessness belong to
those who are cursed by God; kindness and humility and gentleness to those beloved of him.

I. The way of blessedness (31:1–36:6)

31 Let us then cling to his blessing, and let us learn what is

---

Christians should "cling to" (cf. 31:1 and especially 46:1–2) those
whom God favors, and "put on" (a common New Testament expression perhaps based on baptismal practice) concord (ten times in
the letter) in humility and continence (four times, here because of
the list of vices), avoiding "gossip and slander" (Rom. 1:29–30; reproduced in 35:5) and justified by works, not by mere words (Jas.
2:14–26; Clement gives the other aspect of justification in 32:3–4;
see commentary). A quotation from Job 11:2–3 shows that verbosity
is no substitute for piety. Clement sums up his understanding of the
quotation with a phrase from Romans 2:29: "The authentic Jew has
his praise not from men but from God." God hates self-praisers—presumably the rebels at Corinth (38:2). The thought, but not the
expression, of the sentences about self-praise resembles what Paul
says of "boasting" and the Johannine words, "If I glorify myself, my
glory is nothing" (John 8:54). Finally Clement contrasts three
(Corinthian?) vices with three Christian virtues:

arrogance	kindness
self-will	humility
recklessness	gentleness

Those who practice the first have been cursed by God (cf. Rom. 1:18–
31); those who practice the second have been blessed. This point
leads Clement into the examples provided in the next chapter.

31:1–36:6. Since gentleness, humility, and meekness are charac-
teristics of those who have been blessed by God (30:8), Clement
proceeds to (re)consider the "ways" (cf. Did. 1:1–2; Barn. 18:1)
of blessing, passing from the ground of blessing (examples from the
Old Testament, ch. 31) to the greatness of the blessing given Jacob
—because of his faith (ch. 32, with an echo of 31:2). Faith implies
continuance in good works in imitation of the Creator (ch. 33). The
Old Testament itself shows that good works in obedience to God's
will are characteristic of men and angels alike and lead to what God
has promised (chs. 34–35) through Jesus Christ, our high priest (ch.
36). In the last two chapters God's present gifts are mentioned as
anticipations of his gifts to come.

31:1–4. God offers his blessing (30:8); we should "cling" to it or

the way to blessedness. Let us unroll the records of the past.
2. Why was our forefather Abraham blest? Was it not because
he acted in righteousness and dependability through faith? 3.
With confidence Isaac, because he realized what was going to
happen, gladly let himself be led to sacrifice. 4. In humility
Jacob departed from his country because of his brother, and
went to Laban and served him; and there was given him the
twelve scepters of the tribes of Israel.

32 Anyone who will consider this with an open mind will
realize the magnificence of the gifts God has given. 2. For from
Jacob came all the priests and Levites that serve at the altar of
God. From him is descended the Lord Jesus according to the
flesh. From him came the kings and rulers and governors in the
Judaean succession. Nor do his other scepters lack luster, for
God promised, "Your seed shall be as the stars of heaven." 3. So

---

join it—an admonition quite common in Clement's letter (15:1; 19:2;
30:3; 46:4). What are the paths (usually singular in Clement) which
lead to blessing? They can be discovered by unfolding or "poring
over" (Lightfoot p. 97 compares Lucian, *Nigrinus* 7) what took place
from the beginning—in order to find examples, in this instance provided by the patriarchs. (1) Our forefather Abraham (cf. "our
father Jacob," 4:8; also "our fathers," 60:4; 62:2; "our forefather
Isaac," Rom. 9:10) was blessed because he effected "righteousness
and truth" (cf. Tob. 4:6; Eph. 5:9) through faith (a combination,
as Lightfoot p. 97 notes, of Rom. 4:1–3 and Gal. 3:6–10 with Jas.
2:20–24). For Clement, as often for Paul, "faith" is equivalent to
"obedience." (2) Isaac had confidence because of his knowledge of
the future (given him by Abraham, Gen. 22:8) and was glad to be
led forth as a sacrifice (so also Josephus, *Ant.* 1, 232; not in the Old
Testament). (3) Finally, Jacob humbly departed from his country
(as the Corinthian rebels will be asked to depart, 54:2; 55:1) and
after being Laban's slave, was given authority over the twelve tribes
of Israel. (32:1: Details of the Old Testament story prove the greatness of God's gifts to Jacob.)
32:1–4. Clement's argument about God's gifts to Jacob can be
proved in detail. From Jacob come (1) "the priests and Levites that
[still?] serve at the altar of God," (2) "the Lord Jesus according to
the flesh" (cf. Rom. 9:5), (3) "kings and rulers and governors in the
Judaean succession," and (4) "other scepters." The last three points
are based on the prophecy of Jacob in Genesis 49:10: rulers and
governors will not depart from Judah until he comes to whom rule

to all of them came honor and greatness not through themselves nor their deeds nor yet through the righteous action they took, but through his will. 4. So we too, who by his will have been called in Christ Jesus, are justified not of ourselves nor through our own wisdom or understanding or piety, nor yet through the things we have accomplished in purity of heart, but through that faith through which almighty God has justified all men from the beginning, to whom be glory for ever and ever. Amen.

---

belongs. Since the promise that their "seed shall be as the stars of heaven" was given to Abraham (Gen. 15:5; 22:17) and to Isaac (Gen. 26:4), it obviously applied to their descendants.

Because God's gifts were given in consequence of prophecies and promises, they were obviously based not on the recipients' works (= right actions) but on God's own will (cf. Rom. 9:16; Eph. 2:8; 2 Tim. 1:9; Tit. 3:5; also Deut. 9:5). And we who by his will have been called "in Christ Jesus" (as in 38:1 and in Ignatius, this form of the name indicates that the author has Pauline ideas in mind) are not made righteous (1) "of ourselves," or (2) by our "wisdom or understanding" (cf. 1 Cor. 1:19) or "piety" or "the things we have accomplished in purity of heart" but (3) by "faith" (cf. Gal. 2:16; 3:8; 3:24; Sanders p. 154). Indeed, the omnipotent God (he whose will is irresistible) has justified all men by faith always (at least those who have believed since the time of Abraham, Gen. 15:6; Gal. 3:6; Rom. 4:3). Mention of God's act leads Clement to pronounce a doxology (cf. Rom. 9:5 and the commentary on 20:12). As Sanders pp. 151–158 points out, Clement is clearly a follower of Paul—as, it may be added, he also is when he insists on "doing good" in the next chapter.

Nevertheless, the phraseology of the concluding sentence is evidence that Clement, like other followers of Paul, does not always observe the latter's distinctive usages. Clement has "justified . . . through (dia) faith," but with that verb Paul uses "on the ground of" (ek) or, as in Romans 3:28, the simple dative (pistei). "Through faith" Paul customarily used in phrases like "to bring the law to nought through faith" (Rom. 3:31), or "for we walk by faith, not by sight" (2 Cor. 5:7), or "wherefore we are encouraged by your faith" (1 Thess. 3:7). However, dia pisteōs is found in Romans 3:22 and in Galatians 2:16 and 3:26 in the phrase "through the faith of Christ" (cf. 2 Tim. 3:15) and in Colossians 2:12 in the phrase "raised . . . through faith in the working of God." A usage similar to that of Clement is found in Hebrews 6:12, "Who through faith and patient endurance receive the promises."

33 What then should we do, brethren? Should we weary of doing good and desist from the works of love? May the Master never let that happen to us, at any rate, but let us hasten earnestly and eagerly to do "every good work" [Tit. 3:1]. 2. For the Creator and Master of all things himself rejoices in his works. 3. Thus by his almighty power he established the heavens and by his inscrutable wisdom set them in order. The earth he separated from the surrounding seas and fixed upon the sure foundation of his own will. The living creatures roaming upon it he called into being by his decree; the sea and its destined creatures he enclosed by his own power. 4. And finally, with his holy and faultless hands he fashioned man, his pre-eminent and greatest work, the very impress of his image. 5. For thus God spake: "Let us make man according to our image and likeness; and God made man, male and female he created them" [Gen. 1:26–27]. 6. Then when he had finished all these things, he praised them and blessed them and said, "Increase and multiply" [Gen. 1:28]. 7. We should note that all the righteous have been adorned with

---

33:1–8. Justification is by faith alone (32:3–4), but Clement, like Paul, cannot believe that it excludes the practice of "the works of love" (cf. especially Rom. 6:1). Idleness is no virtue; readiness for "every good work" (Tit. 3:1; 2 Tim. 2:21; 3:17; 2 Cor. 9:8) is indispensable. Knopf p. 98 criticizes Clement for combining "synergism" with "solafideism" and compares his remarks about Abraham's works in 31:2 (cf. Jas. 2:20–24). Actually Clement is insisting upon the imitation of God who is Creator as well as Redeemer. He proceeds to describe the work of creation as due to God's supreme might, his incomprehensible intelligence, his will, his decree, and his power; compare the panegyric in Hermas, Visions 1, 3, 4 (Hermas concludes with the Church, Clement with man). The climax is reached with man, most excellent and supreme because of his intelligence, whom God fashioned with his "holy and faultless hands" (cf. Gen. 2:7) as the imprint (cf. Heb. 1:3) of his image (cf. 2 Cor. 3:18). Genesis 1:26–28 proves that man was intended to imitate God's creative activity. Righteous men have done so (chs. 31–32); the Lord (God) himself "adorned" (*kosmēsas*; cf. the *kosmos* of Gen. 2:1) himself with good works (of creation) and rejoiced (rested, Gen. 2:2). Since we have this "example" (16:17; cf. 5:7) we should "accede to his will" (as disciples, cf. 63:1) and work "with all our might" (Deut. 6:5; cf. Matt. 22:37; Mark 12:33; Luke 10:27).

On early Christian quotations of Genesis 1:26 see Hatch pp. 142–143.

good works, just as even the Lord adorned himself with good
works and rejoiced. 8. Consequently, since we have this example,
let us accede to his will without hesitation; let us endeavor with
all our might to do the works of righteousness.

34 The good workman accepts the bread he has earned with
rightful self-assurance; the lazy and careless one cannot look
his employer in the face. 2. So must we be eager to do what is
good, since all things come from him. 3. For he warns us, "Behold the Lord [is coming], and his reward is before him, and he
will pay every man according to his work" [Isa. 40:10]. 4. He
urges us, then, if we believe in him with our whole heart not to
be idle or careless in "any good work" [Tit. 3:1]. 5. Let our
boast and our assurance be in him; let us be subject to his will;
let us consider how the whole company of the angels stands

34:1–8. In this chapter Clement continues to speak of the necessity of good works and of being a good workman (like the one mentioned in Matt. 10:10, worthy of his food) who can look his employer
in the face. Both glory and punishment come from God, who warns
men in advance—with a quotation either from a lost document or
from a mixture of Isaiah 40:10; 62:11; Proverbs 24:12, and (perhaps) other passages (cf. Knopf p. 102). Wholehearted faith involves
being ready "for every good work" (cf. Tit. 3:1, etc.; *The New
Testament in the Apostolic Fathers* [Oxford, 1905], 51). Our glorying
(cf. 13:1, with Pauline reminiscences) and confidence (35:2; cf. van
Unnik p. 223) are to be in him; we are to submit to his will by doing
good works. We should consider the (example provided by) the
host of angels who stand by him and serve his will. Two texts (combined under the heading "the scripture says") prove that this is so.
(1) Daniel 7:10 shows that myriads of angels stood by him and
thousands served him; (2) Isaiah 6:3 proves that though there were
so many, they praised him unanimously (van Unnik pp. 228–229).
Therefore Christians must be brought together in harmony by com-
pliance with the will of God (van Unnik pp. 229–234), and cry out to
God for his aid so that they may have a share in his promises.
Finally such a promise is stated, either from an apocryphal book or
from Isaiah 64:4 and 65:16–17; see P. Prigent, "Ce que l'oeil n'a
pas vu, I Cor 2, 9," in *Theologische Zeitschrift* 14 (1958), 416–429.
    The references above to the article by W. C. van Unnik (*Vigiliae
Christianae* 5 [1951], 204–248) indicate that we agree with him (1)
that there is no liturgical reference in this chapter, and (2) that the
context of Clement's thought is eschatological, not cultic. The quotation of Isaiah 6:3 proves nothing whatever about the place of the

ready to serve his will. 6. For the Scripture says, "Ten thousand times ten thousand stood by him, and thousands of thousands ministered to him, and they cried out, 'Holy, holy, holy is the Lord of Hosts; the whole creation is full of his glory'" [Dan. 7:10; Isa. 6:3]. 7. Let us then also be assembled in concord [cf. Ps. 82:6], with full consciousness of our duty, and cry to him earnestly as with one voice [Greek, "mouth"], that we may share in his great and glorious promises. 8. For it says, "Eye has not seen nor ear heard nor has there entered into the heart of man, what things he has prepared for those who patiently wait for him" [1 Cor. 2:9; Isa. 64:4; 65:16–17].

35 How blessed and wonderful are the gifts of God, beloved! 2. Life in immortality, splendor in righteousness, truth in boldness, faith in confidence, self-control in holiness; and all these fall within our comprehension. 3. What things, then, are being

---

Sanctus in the early Christian Eucharist, for which there is no evidence before the middle of the fourth century.

Indeed, we should perhaps incline to suppose that the texts from Daniel and Isaiah were taken by Clement from an anthology, to which he leads up with the words "stand ready" and "serve" (*leitourgousin*). Both words occur in the quotation from Daniel, but "served" (*eleitourgoun*) is found only in Theodotion's version, not in the Septuagint. Since Clement seems to be using the Septuagint, not Theodotion, when he summarizes Daniel for himself in 45:6–7, we may suggest that the quotation of Daniel 7:10 here is not his own.

The phraseology of verse 3 is a striking illustration of the conflation of texts. Clement has: *Idou ho Kyrios, kai ho misthos autou pro prosōpou autou, apodounai hekastōi kata to ergon autou.* The first phrase, but without the article, is found at the beginning of Isaiah 40:10 and 62:11. *Ho misthos autou* is in 40:10; *pro prosōpou autou* in 62:11. The last phrase is found in substance in Proverbs 24:12, Psalm 61:13b, Revelation 22:12, and Matthew 16:27. But to get Clement's wording exactly, one has to take *apodounai hekastōi* from Revelation 22:12, *kata* from Proverbs, Psalms, or Matthew, and *to ergon autou* from Revelation (though Proverbs, Psalms and some MSS of Matthew have *ta erga*). The passage from Psalm 61 is quoted also in Romans 2:6 (*apodōsei hekastōi kata ta erga autou*). Evidently Clement is "quoting" from memory.

35:1–7. What has God prepared for those who wait for him (34:8)? His gifts, "blessed" and "wonderful" (cf. 26:1; 50:1), are already in part known to us; Clement describes them in five short rhetorical cola. But there are gifts which we do not yet know (as

prepared for those who wait for him? The Creator and Father
of the ages, the all holy One himself knows their greatness and
beauty. 4. Let us therefore strive to be in the number of those
that wait for him, so that we may share in the promised gifts.
5. And how shall this be, beloved? If our mind is fixed faithfully upon God, if we seek out what is well pleasing and acceptable to him, if we accomplish what is in accord with his
faultless will and follow in the way of truth; if we cast away
from ourselves "all manner of wickedness, evil, covetousness,"
strife, "malignity and deceit, gossip and slander, hatred of God,
haughtiness and boastfulness," vanity and inhospitality. 6. For
"those who practice such things are hateful to God"; and "not
only those who themselves practice them, but also those who
approve their doing so" [Rom. 1:29–32 paraphrased]. 7. For the
Scripture says,

"But to the sinner God said:
    'What right have you to recite my statutes,
    or take my covenant on your lips?
For you have hated discipline,
    and have cast my words behind you.
If you saw a thief, you were a friend of his;

---

stated in 34:8). Only the one who created the ages—this age and
the one to come (van Unnik p. 242)—knows how great they are and
how beautiful they are. The epithet "Father of the ages" is paralleled
by "the eternal God" (55:6) and "King of the ages" (61:2), also
"Father of the universe" (19:2; Knopf p. 105). "All holy" occurs in
58:1 and the Hellenistic Jewish 4 Maccabees (7:4; 14:7). Christians
must "contest" or "strive" to be found among the "number" (2:4;
58:2; 59:2) of those who wait for God, and for his gifts.

Therefore their minds must be fixed through faith upon God and
they must follow the "way of truth" (cf. 31:1; 35:12; 36:1). They
follow by rejecting all sorts of vices, paraphrased from Romans 1:29–
32 (on the text cf. G. Zuntz, *The Text of the Epistles* [Oxford, 1953],
219–220), and by agreeing with evildoers—as described in "the
Scripture" (Ps. 49:16–23). The main point is reached in the last
verse of the quotation: "Praise as a sacrifice will honor me, and that
is the way in which I will show him the salvation of God" (cf. 52:3).

An interesting variant is to be found in verse 11 (Psalm 49:22).
Neither in the Hebrew nor in most manuscripts of the Septuagint
does any reference to a lion occur; it is to be found, however, in the
sixth-century Graeco-Latin Psalter at Verona, used in H. B. Swete's
edition of the Septuagint.

and you kept company with adulterers.
You have given your mouth free rein for evil,
   and your tongue has framed deceit.
You sat and spake against your brother;
   you slandered your own mother's son.
These things you have done and I have been silent;
   you thought, lawless one, that I would be like yourself.
But I will rebuke you and lay the charge before you.'

Mark this, then, you who forget God,
   lest he rend like a lion, and there be none to deliver!
Praise as a sacrifice will honor me;
   and that is the way in which
I will show the salvation of God!" [Ps. 49:16–23].

36 This is the way, beloved, in which we found our salvation, Jesus Christ, the high priest of our offerings, the protector and helper of our weakness [cf. Heb. 2:17; 3:1; 4:15].
2. Through him we fix our eyes on the heights of heaven,
   Through him we see mirrored the flawless and sublime countenance of God [cf. 2 Cor. 3:18],

---

36:1–6. Clement now explains the meaning of the "way of truth" (35:5; cf. 48:2–4), the "way" mentioned in Psalm 49:23. The way is not Jesus, as in John 14:6; it is the way in which God's salvation (Ps. 49:23) has been found—and Jesus Christ is this salvation (cf. 1 Cor. 1:30). He is the high priest (Heb. 2:17, etc.; Ignatius, Philad. 9:1; Polycarp, Phil. 12:2; Mart. Polyc. 14:3; Justin, *Dialogue* 33:2, etc.; other references in Lightfoot p. 111; Knopf p. 106) who makes offerings for Christians (cf. 44:4); he is their defender or guardian (61:3; ch. 64) and helper (59:3–4; cf. Heb. 2:18) of their weakness (Heb. 4:15). Obviously Clement is relying on Hebrews for this description, but before quoting it further, he provides a rhetorical account of the work of revelation through Christ: five cola beginning with "through him," two emphasizing what is seen, two speaking of that which sees, and one referring to taste. The Christian sees the heights of heaven (cf. 49:4; 59:3) and the reflection of God's countenance (cf. Wisd. 7:26; 2 Cor. 3:18); the eyes of his heart are opened (cf. 59:3) and his "foolish and darkened understanding" (cf. Rom. 1:21 and recall use of Rom. 1:29–32 in 35:5–6) "springs up" toward the light. The Master (God) willed that through Christ we should "taste immortal knowledge" (cf. 35:2; Did. 9:3; 10:2; for tasting cf. Heb. 6:4–5). Knopf p. 107 suggests that this

Through him the eyes of our heart have been opened,

Through him our foolish and darkened understanding springs
    up to the light,

Through him the Master has willed that we should taste im-
    mortal knowledge;

For "since he is the express image of his greatness, he is as
    much superior to angels as his title is superior" to theirs
    [cf. Heb. 1:3-4].

3. For thus it is written, "He makes his angels wings and his
ministers a flame of fire" [Ps. 103:4; Heb. 1:7]. 4. But concerning his Son the Master spoke thus, "Thou art my son, this day
have I begotten thee; ask of me, and I shall give the nations for
thine inheritance and the ends of the earth for thy possession"
[Ps. 2:7-8; Heb. 1:5]. 5. And again he says to him, "Sit thou
on my right hand until I make thy enemies the footstool of thy
feet" [Ps. 109:1; Heb. 1:13]. 6. Who then are the enemies? Those
who are wicked and resist his will.

J. Conclusion (37:1–39:9)

37 Let us then, men and brethren, engage in our service with
complete earnestness under his faultless order. 2. Let us consider those who serve under our military commanders, with what
good discipline, subordination, and obedience they carry out

language is liturgical, but not all rhetoric is necessarily related to
liturgy. Through Christ the eye sees and the ear hears (cf. 34:8).

Now (vs. 4) Clement turns directly to speak of Christ in language
taken from Hebrews 1:3-4, 7, 5, 13. He expands the Hebrews quotation from Psalm 2:7 by adding to it the next verse in the psalm. The
enemies of God (Ps. 109:1) are identified as "those who are wicked
and resist his will"; as Knopf p. 108 suggests, this is an illusion to the
"disobedient" at Corinth.

G. Zuntz has discussed Clement's text of Hebrews in *The Text of
the Epistles* (Oxford, 1953), 218. He believes that Clement's repeated phrase "through him" is based on the reading of "through
himself" (*di' hautou*) at the end of Hebrews 1:3, as in the Beatty
papyri (P 46); with this corresponds Clement's omission of "the" in
"the angels" (Heb. 1:4).

37:1-39:9. Because of the greatness of God's promises to those
who join Christ against his enemies (36:5-6), Christians must un-
dergo "our service" and observe its discipline (37:1-3); they must
recognize that great and small are "mixed" (37:4) as in the human
body (37:5) which is analogous to "our body" (the Church, though

orders. 3. Not all are prefects or tribunes or centurions or captains of fifty and so on, but "each in his own rank" [1 Cor. 15: 23] carries out orders under the emperor and the commanding officers. 4. The great cannot exist without the small; neither can the small exist without the great: there is a certain mutuality in the whole, and this is beneficial to it. 5. Take, for example, our body: the head is nothing without the feet, just as the feet are nothing without the head; "and the least members of the body

---

Clement does not explicitly say so; his correspondents know 1 Corinthians; 38:1) with its mutuality of concern (38:2) and its common dependence on God (38:3–4). Old Testament texts prove that man is as nothing compared with his Creator; therefore self-exaltation is absurd (ch. 39).

37:1–5. Because of God's gifts we should maintain military discipline—a theme popular in the Hellenistic-Roman diatribe and, as Knopf p. 108 observes, common among Christians since the time of Paul (cf. 2 Cor. 10:3; 1 Tim. 1:18; 2 Tim. 2:3–4; Ignatius, Polyc. 6:2; Lightfoot p. 113). Clement combines the military motif with ideas derived from 1 Corinthians 12 and 15. But is it derived from meditation about the Roman army? It is far more likely that it is based on Jewish precedents, for in the Roman army there was no "captain of fifty"; instead, the list of officers which Clement provides is close to that given in Exodus 18:21, 25 and re-established by Judas Maccabaeus (1 Macc. 3:55) and in the Dead Sea War Scroll (col. III, line 17). The Hellenistic Jewish general Josephus mentions the "captains of fifty" when he paraphrases Exodus (*Ant.* 3, 71) but not when he paraphrases 1 Maccabees (*Ant.* 12, 301) or when he describes the organization of his own command in Roman fashion (*Bell.* 2, 578). On this subject see Y. Yadin, *The Scroll of the War of the Sons of Light Against the Sons of Darkness* (Oxford, 1962), 59. Clement is not, therefore, "pointing . . . to the parallel of the Roman army and its hierarchic discipline" (Jaeger p. 19); as usual, he has the Old Testament in mind. See 41:1, where the expression "in his own rank" (1 Cor. 15:23) recurs.

This is not to say that he confines his attention to Old Testament ideas. The notions about the small and the great and the "mixture" in everything are based, as Jaeger pp. 19–20 rightly points out, on commonplaces probably derived from Sophocles (*Ajax* 158) and Euripides (*Aiolos*, frag. 21), no doubt by way of a Stoic source (so Jaeger p. 116).

The word *synkrasis* may well be based on 1 Corinthians 12:24 (Lightfoot p. 115). Finally Clement turns directly to 1 Corinthians 12:21–23, in which are set forth the mutual relations of head and feet, as well as the importance of the "weaker" (Clement substitutes "least") members of the body. All "breathe together" or coalesce (be-

are necessary and useful to the whole body" [cf. 1 Cor. 12:21-22]; but they all coalesce and are alike subordinated for the health of the body as a whole.

38 So let our whole body be preserved in Christ Jesus [cf. Eph. 5:21], and let each put himself at the service of his neighbor as his particular spiritual gift dictates. 2. Let the strong care for the weak, and let the weak respect the strong. Let the rich provide for the poor, and let the poor give thanks to God because he has given him one through whom his needs are met. Let the wise man show his wisdom not in words but in [ap-

---

cause of the one Spirit of 1 Cor. 12:4–13; Paul says "suffer together" and "rejoice together," 1 Cor. 12:26) and make use of a common obedience (cf. Eph. 5:21; 1 Pet. 5:5). Knopf's complaint (pp. 109–110) that "the mystical truth" about the "one body in Christ" is lacking in 1 Clement is due partly to his mistranslation of "breathe together" as "sind *einmütig*" (cf. Jaeger p. 22), and partly to his notion that Clement should simply have reproduced what Paul wrote. Furthermore, Clement is just about to repeat his reference to preserving the whole body—in Christ Jesus (38:1).

38:1–4.   Clement has just spoken of preserving the "whole body" (37:5); now, as not elsewhere in his letter except in 46:7, where he is also relying on 1 Corinthians, he again advocates preserving the whole body by being subordinate to one's neighbor (Eph. 5:21; Rom. 15:2) in relation to the position of each in accordance with his gift of grace (1 Cor. 12:4–11, 28–31; cf. also Rom. 12:3–8). The idea that the "strong" should care for the "weak" and that each should be concerned for his neighbor is based upon Romans 15:1–2; Clement's notion that the "weak" should "respect the strong" is based on his own idea of order and also is implied by Paul's words. The explicit counsel for the rich man to help the poor man and for the poor man to give thanks to God is evidently characteristic of Roman Christian practice; it is elaborately worked out in Hermas, Similitudes 2, 5–7. The fact that something quite similar is found in fragments of Sophocles and Euripides (Knopf p. 109; Jaeger pp. 19–20) shows only that traditional wisdom tends to be expressed in similar ways in various cultures. Deeds are more important than words, as in 30:3. One should not bear witness to one's own virtue (30:6–7). We must not boast of purity or continence, for it is a gift of God (Gal. 5:23; cf. Ignatius, Polyc. 5:2).

Men must bear their creaturely status in mind by considering "of what sort of stuff" (substance; i.e., earth, 39:2) they originated, of what sort and who they were as they were brought into the world from a "grave and darkness" (Knopf p. 111 well compares the

propriate] good deeds. Let the humble not draw attention to himself, but leave it to others to speak well of him. Let him who is continent not boast of it, but be mindful that it is another who bestows upon him his self-control. 3. So let us all bear in mind, brethren, of what sort of stuff we are made, who we are, and what kind of beings we came into this world, out of what grave and darkness our Creator and Master brought us into this world, having prepared his benefits for us before we were born. 4. Since we have all these things from him, we ought to give thanks to him in everything; to whom be the glory for ever and ever. Amen.

39 Foolish, senseless, stupid, and ignorant men mock and scorn us, in a conceited effort to exalt themselves. 2. For what can a mortal man do? What strength has earth-born man? 3. For it is written,

"There was no form before my eyes,
but I heard a breeze and a voice.

---

language of Ps. 138:15). Sometimes the questions raised here are thought to be "Gnostic," and so they are in Clement, *Excerpta ex Theodoto* 78, 2; but here, in 2 Clement 1:2–3, and in Barnabas 14:5–7 there is no reason for so regarding them. They are semi-philosophical in nature and that is why some Gnostics asked them.

Since God is the source of everything (1 Cor. 8:6; Rom. 11:36, etc.) Christians must give him thanks and glory; Clement sums up with a doxology.

39:1–9. The doxology in 38:4 leaves Clement free to attack his opponents, presumably those at Corinth, and he uses Pauline invective (chiefly from 1 Corinthians) to criticize their lack of intelligence both innate and due to their lack of education. They fail to recognize that they are mortal and (like Adam) born from the earth—as a quotation from the book of Job makes plain. This quotation is interesting because of its composite character. It begins with the Septuagint text of Job 4:16–18. But Job 4:17–18 is closely paralleled by Job 15:14–13–15a, and Clement next proceeds to quote Job 15:15b. The words "let alone" occur in Job 15:16 and in Codex Alexandrinus at the beginning of Job 4:19. Clement provides a quotation from Job 4:19–5:5. This is very close to the Septuagint except for the last line or so. Job 5:5 reads, "What they gathered, the righteous will eat." Clement, using a text apparently Christianized (see 13:1; 15:2), reads, "What was prepared for them" (cf. Mark 10:40; Matt. 20:23).

4. What! Can a mortal be pure before the Lord?
   Or can a man be blameless for his actions,
if he has no confidence
   even in his servants
   and even in his angels finds some fault?
5. Not even heaven is pure in his sight,
   let alone those who dwell in houses of clay
   of whom are we ourselves, made of the same clay.
He smote them like a moth
   and they did not survive from morning to evening,
   because they could not help themselves they perished.
6. He breathed on them,
   and they died because they had no wisdom.
7. Call out and see if anyone will hear you,
   or if you will see any of the holy angels.
For wrath destroys the stupid
   and jealousy brings death to one deceived.
8. I have seen the foolish taking root
   but their dwelling was suddenly consumed.
9. May their sons be far from safety!
   Let them be mocked at the doors of lesser men,
   and there will be none to deliver them.
For what was prepared for them shall the righteous eat
   and they themselves shall not be delivered from evil"
   [Job 4:16–18; 15:15; 4:19–5:5].

III. Solution for the Corinthians' problem (40:1–61:3)

A. The divine origin of church order (40:1–44:6)

40 Now then, since this is quite plain to us, and we have gained insight into the depths of the divine knowledge [cf. Rom. 11:33; 1 Cor. 2:10], we ought to do in order all those things the Master has ordered us to perform at the appointed times. 2. He

---

40:1–44:6.   In this small but crucial section on the divine origin of church order, the author interweaves materials relating to order in the Old Testament (chs. 40–41; 43) with those bearing directly upon

has commanded sacrifices and services to be performed, not in a careless and haphazard way but at the designated seasons and hours. 3. He himself has determined where and through whom he wishes them performed, to the intent that everything should be done religiously to his good pleasure and acceptably to his

---

the Christians' apostolic succession (chs. 42; 44). Previously he has mentioned "each in his own rank" (a phrase derived verbally from 1 Cor. 15:23) only with reference to the army (37:3); now it occurs in regard to the Church (41:1). Chapter 40 is full of references to "order" or "appointment" (six times), to "decrees" (twice), and to "services" (twice). Clement uses the sacrificial ordinances of the Old Testament to prepare the ground for his defense of ordinances (which he must regard as analogous) in regard to the Church. The Aaronic high priest (43:5; cf. 40:5; 41:2) has been superseded by "the high priest of our offerings" (36:1), but Clement does not say so—because he has already said so, and will say so again (61:3; ch. 64).

40:1–5. What is "quite plain" to us—the "depths of the divine knowledge" (cf. 1 Cor. 2:10, "the depths of God")—consists of the whole argument up to this point, based on the Old Testament revelation and confirmed by the teaching of Christ and the apostle Paul. (Clement can speak indiscriminately of "depths," cf. 2:2, and "height," 49:4; 59:3.) He now turns to his "political" argument about the necessity of order as derived from God, who commanded worship to be performed at fixed seasons and hours, in fixed places, and by duly appointed persons. His remarks apply to "services" (*leitourgiai*) in general and to "offerings" or "sacrifices" (*prosphorai*) in particular. At the end of this chapter it becomes clear that Clement's ideas are derived not so much from 1 Corinthians (11:34b; 14:33, 40) as from the Old Testament cultus, where he finds different duties assigned to the high priest, the priests in general, the Levites, and the people; he uses the adjective *laikos* simply to indicate someone who is not a priest or a Levite, though it is quite evident that the "layman" has a function different from theirs, as well as a different and lower rank (cf. 37:1–3; 41:1). On words referring to rank, especially in 1 Peter 5:2–3 (and in Clement), see W. Nauck in *Zeitschrift für die neutestamentliche Wissenschaft* 48 (1957), 200–220.

His statements about temple worship do not show us whether or not he regards it as still continuing after the (partial) destruction of the Temple in A.D. 70. It is possible that in fact it did continue, but his purpose is to show that the arrangements for it were of divine origin.

High priest, priests, and Levites may not correspond exactly to Jesus, our high priest (36:1; 61:3; ch. 64), presbyter-bishops, and deacons (chs. 42; 44), but the analogy could hardly escape any

will. 4. Those then who offer their sacrifices at the appointed
seasons are acceptable and blessed; for since they comply with
the Master's orders, they do not sin. 5. Thus to the high priest
have been appointed his proper services, to the priests their own
place assigned, upon the Levites their proper duties imposed;
and the layman is bound by the rules for laymen.

41 Each of us, brethren, in his own rank [cf. 1 Cor. 15:23] must
please God in good conscience, not overstepping the fixed rules
of his ministry, and with reverence. 2. Not everywhere, brethren,
but in Jerusalem only are the perpetual sacrifices [cf. Exod.
29:38 ff.; Num. 28:3 ff.] offered, whether thank offering or those
for sin and trespass; and even there they are not offered in every
place, but only in front of the sanctuary, at the altar, after the

---

reader who was paying attention to Clement's text (Knopf's asser-
tion, p. 114, to the contrary). For the bishop as priest or high priest
see my article in *Catholic Biblical Quarterly* 25 (1963), 330–331.

41:1–4. What it means to please God in one's rank and not to
transgress the appointed rule (cf. the cosmic examples in ch. 20) of
his service is made clear in what follows. The Old Testament makes
it very clear that a regular procedure is to be followed in regard to
daily sacrifices, freewill offerings, sin offerings, and trespass offerings
(on these cf. Knopf p. 115). Clement does not really care much
about the offerings as such; he is concerned only to point out that
they are to be made (1) only at Jerusalem and only before the
temple at the altar, and (2) only after inspection by the high priest
and the other ministers. Violation of these regulations results in the
death penalty (cf. Lev. 17:4; Deut. 13:11, 16, etc.).

The fact that greater knowledge brings greater risk (cf. 40:1)
must mean that the situation of the Christians is analogous to and
continuous with that of the Hebrews. Therefore Clement must be
saying that Christian worship cannot be conducted in private as-
semblies apart from the bishops, presbyters, and deacons whom he is
about to discuss. Knopf p. 114 rightly compares Ignatius, Smyrnaeans
8:1: "Apart from the bishop no one is to do anything pertaining to
the Church." And as Ignatius there says that Jesus Christ follows
the Father, so here Clement is about to point out that he was sent
from God. In their different ways both Clement and Ignatius base
church order on the relation of Christ to the Father and the apostles
to Christ.

Is the temple cultus still being carried on? K. W. Clark (*New
Testament Studies* 6 [1959–60], 269–280) has adduced Christian
and Jewish sources which suggest that it was not terminated until

offering has been inspected by the high priest and the aforemen-
tioned ministers. 3. Further, those who do anything contrary to
the duty imposed by his will incur the death penalty. 4. Understand then, brethren: the greater the knowledge that has been
bestowed upon us, the greater the risk we run.

42 The apostles received the gospel for us from Jesus Christ,
and Jesus the Christ was sent from God. 2. So Christ is from
God, and the apostles are from Christ: thus both came in proper
order by the will of God. 3. And so the apostles, after they had
received their orders and in full assurance by reason of the resurrection of our Lord Jesus Christ, being full of faith in the
word of God, went out in the conviction of the Holy Spirit
preaching the good news that God's kingdom was about to come.
4. So as they preached from country to country and from city to
city, they appointed their first converts, after testing them by the
Spirit, to be the bishops and deacons of the future believers.
5. Nor was this an innovation; since bishops and deacons had

A.D. 135. We may question his dating of Hebrews in the reign of
Domitian, but that is the time of both Clement and Josephus (*C.
Apionem* 2, 77; 2, 193–198), and the Christian additions to 2 Esdras
(perhaps about 100) speak of sacrifices as continuing (1:31). Clement's language certainly tends to confirm Clark's argument.

42:1–5. Clement now makes an abrupt transition as he passes
from the more static or prefigurative picture of the ministry (as Jaeger
suggested) to the historical actuality. God sent Jesus Christ, who in
turn gave the gospel to the apostles; therefore both Christ and the
apostles were produced "in proper order" from or by the will of God
(cf. Ignatius, Smyrn. 8:1). The orderliness of apostolic order thus
serves to prove its divine origin. The apostles were "in full assurance"
(Luke 1:1) by the resurrection (cf. Acts 1:3; 2:36) and had their
faith confirmed by the word of God (cf. Luke 24:27, 44–46); then
they went forth with assurance provided by the Holy Spirit (1 Thess.
1:5; cf. Acts 2:4) to proclaim the future coming of the kingdom of
God (Luke 19:11; 24:21; Acts 1:6–8). They preached in rural (Acts
8:1) and urban areas (Acts, *passim*), and appointed their "first
fruits" (earliest converts, 1 Cor. 16:15; Rom. 16:5), after testing them
by the Spirit (cf. 1 Tim. 3:10) as bishops and deacons (cf. Phil.
1:1; also an inference from 1 Cor. 16:16?). For the appointment of
presbyters in various churches see Acts 14:23; in various cities, Titus
1:5.

In order to link his Christian history with Old Testament prophecy,

been written of long before. For thus says the Scripture somewhere, "I will appoint their bishops in righteousness and their
deacons in faith" [Isa. 60:17, modified].

43 And is it any wonder, if those who in Christ were entrusted
by God with such a duty should appoint those just mentioned?
For when the blessed Moses, too, "a faithful servant in all the
house" [Num. 12:7; Heb. 3:2, 5] wrote in the sacred books all
that had been commanded him, the rest of the prophets became

Clement provides a rather forced quotation from "the Scripture somewhere" (perhaps a collection of testimonies?)—actually Isaiah 60:17:

I will appoint their bishops	I will give your rulers (*archontas*)
in righteousness	in peace
and their deacons	and your overseers (*episkopous*)
in faith	in righteousness

Irenaeus (*Adv. haer.* 4, 26, 5) also refers the verse to the Christian
ministry but manages to quote the Septuagint correctly. On Clement's
text see Hatch p. 179.

The idea of quoting the Old Testament for apostolic succession
may come to Clement from Acts 1:20, since a good deal of his ma-
terial about the ministry and its history seems to come from Acts (see
commentary on ch. 5).

43:1–6.   The establishment of the Aaronic priesthood confirms the
divine establishment of the Christian ministry; it was recorded by the
"blessed" Moses, "a faithful servant in all the house" (Num. 12:7;
cf. 1 Clem. 17:5; Heb. 3:5). The word "blessed" is used of God's
gifts in 35:1, but it occurs most frequently in this discussion of church
order (40:4, priests; 44:5, presbyters; 47:1, Paul; 48:4; 50:5, Christians; 50:6; 56:6, quotations from Psalms; 55:4, Judith). The other
prophets (cf. Deut. 18:15; Acts 3:21; 7:37) also bore witness to
Moses' laws (cf. Mal. 4:4).

Clement does not copy the story of the priesthood from Numbers
17 (in spite of his mention of "the sacred books") but paraphrases
it in a manner reminiscent of Philo, *De Vita Mosis* 2, 174–180 or
Josephus, *Antiquities* 4, 63–66 (cf. his paraphrase of Joshua 2 in
ch. 12 and of Judith and Esther in ch. 55). Jealousy arose over the
priesthood and the tribes quarreled (so Philo, *ibid.*, 174; Josephus,
ibid., 66). Moses therefore ordered the rulers to bring him twelve
rods with the name of a tribe (so Josephus, *ibid.*, 63; a ruler, Philo,
ibid., 178) on each. Clement himself (or the kind of rabbinic tradition he is following) adds that Moses sealed them with the rings of
the rulers, put them on "the table of God," and sealed the keys of
the tabernacle. The story thus comes to resemble a Hellenistic miracle

his successors to testify with him to his legislation. 2. For he himself, when strife arose over the priesthood and the tribes were in rebellion over the question which one of them should be adorned with the glorious title, commanded the twelve tribal chiefs to bring to him the staffs inscribed with the name of each tribe. Then he took them and tied them together and sealed them with the rings of the chiefs, and deposited them in the tent of the testimony on the table of God. 3. Then when he had shut the tent he sealed the keys as he had the staffs, 4. and said to the chiefs, "Men and brethren, the tribe whose staff buds is the one God has chosen for his priesthood and ministry." 5. So early in the morning he summoned all Israel, six hundred thousand men, and showed the seals to the tribal chiefs and opened the tent of the testimony and produced the staffs; and the staff of Aaron was found not only to have budded but to be bearing fruit. 6. What do you think, beloved? Did not Moses know in advance that this would happen? Of course he knew. But he acted as he did lest there be an insurrection in Israel and in order that the name of the true and only God might be glorified; to whom be the glory for ever and ever. Amen.

44 And our apostles knew through our Lord Jesus Christ that there would be strife over the title of bishop. 2. So for this reason, because they had been given full foreknowledge, they ap-

---

tale like that of water changed into wine in the locked temple at Elis (Pausanias 6, 26; cf. R. M. Grant, *Miracle and Natural Law* [Amsterdam, 1952], 179). Clement's one "direct quotation" begins with a term of address ("men and brethren") fairly common in Acts (see commentary on 14:1) ascribed to Moses, whereas its model in Numbers 17:5 is ascribed to God. The rhetorical question "Do you think . . . did not Moses know . . .?" is based on Clement's own version of the story; in Numbers it is clear that Moses did know.

The chapter ends with mention of glorifying the name of "the true and only God" (cf. John 17:3) and a doxology.

44:1–6. Christian apostles (in view of the context, like God's emissary Moses) knew through our Lord Jesus Christ that there would be strife over the episcopate. For this knowledge one might think of such predictions as those in Acts 20:29–30; Jude 18; 2 Peter 2:1–3; 1 Timothy 4:1–3; and 2 Timothy 3:1–9; 4:3–4. But these are not explicitly ascribed to Jesus, and one should probably also consider Mark 13:22 and parallel passages as well. Since (like Moses, 43:6)

pointed those mentioned above and afterward added the stipu-
lation that if these should die, other approved men should
succeed to their ministry. 3. Those therefore who were appointed
by them or afterward by other reputable men with the consent
of the whole Church, who in humility have ministered to the
flock of Christ blamelessly, quietly, and unselfishly, and who
have long been approved by all—these men we consider are being unjustly removed from their ministry. 4. Surely we will be
guilty of no small sin if we thrust out of the office of bishop those
who have offered the gifts in a blameless and holy fashion. 5.
Blessed indeed are the presbyters who have already passed on,
who had a fruitful and perfect departure, for they need not be
concerned lest someone remove them from the place established
for them. 6. But you, we observe, have removed some who were
conducting themselves well from the ministry they have ir-
reproachably honored.

B. The opposition of the wicked (45:1–46:9)

45 Be emulous, brethren, and in eager rivalry about the things
that pertain to salvation. 2. Study the sacred scriptures, which
are true and given by the Holy Spirit. 3. Bear in mind that
nothing wrong or falsified is written in them. You will not find

---

they had foreknowledge, they (1) appointed bishops and deacons
("those mentioned above," 42:4) and (2) later added the codicil
(reading *epinomen*) that other "approved" men (for tests cf. 1 Tim.
3:1–12) should succeed to their ministry.

Since present ministers derive their office by succession from the
apostles and, indeed, from God (42:1), appointees either apostolic
or subapostolic—approved by the whole Church, serving Christ's
flock (cf. 16:1; 54:2; 57:2; Acts 20:28; 1 Pet. 5:2) in suitable
fashion, attested for a long time by all—cannot be removed from
their function of offering Christian sacrifices. These sacrifices are
sacrifices of praise and thanksgiving (18:17; 35:12–36:1; 41:1; 52:3;
Heb. 13:15–16; cf. Did. 14).

The presbyters (evidently equivalent to bishops) who have already died are blessed because no one will try to depose them. On
the other hand, at Corinth some presbyters have been unjustly de-
posed. Clement does not tell us how or why.

45:1–46:9. Since church order is based upon God's plan and expresses it (chs. 40–44), only the wicked have persecuted or, more
precisely, driven out the righteous; God defends those who serve
him (ch. 45). We are bound to follow the examples of the righteous

that upright men have ever been thrust out by holy men. 4. The
upright have been persecuted, to be sure, but by the lawless;
they have been imprisoned, but by the impious; they have been
stoned, but by transgressors; they have been slain, but by such
as have been possessed by a depraved and unjust jealousy. 5.
Yet they endured gloriously the suffering of such things. 6. What
indeed can we say, brethren? That Daniel was cast into the den
of lions by men who feared God? [Dan. 6:16-17.] 7. That
Ananias and Azariah and Mishael were shut up in the fiery
furnace by men who practiced the exalted and glorious worship of the Most High? [Dan. 3:19-21.] Certainly not! Who
then were the men who did such things? Hateful men and full
of all wickedness, who carried their factiousness to such a pitch
of fury that they tortured those who were serving God with holy

---

sufferers, not tearing the Christian community apart, and remembering the words of Jesus about the fate of anyone who offends his
elect. Actually, Clement suddenly points out, the continuing
Corinthian schism and sedition has damaged the whole Church (ch.
46).

45:1-2. The word "contentious" or "emulous" (*philoneikoi*) occurs only here in the Apostolic Fathers; it is found in a bad sense in
1 Corinthians 11:16, as is the cognate noun in Martyrdom of Polycarp
18:1. With Lightfoot and others we should treat it here as in a good
sense, leading on to other imperative statements. The Corinthians
must study what pertains to salvation—and is found in the "sacred
scriptures" (53:1; 62:3), trustworthy and inspired.

45:3-8. Since these scriptures were inspired by the Holy Spirit,
one can learn even from what they do not say; and they do not say
that the righteous (or the presbyters at Corinth) have been cast out
by holy or pious men (or the Corinthian community). Clement provides a vividly rhetorical summary of the examples of the righteous
persecuted by the wicked which seems to be based on what he has
set forth in chapters 4-6. Then with the rhetorical question, "What
indeed can we say, brethren?" he turns to further Old Testament examples, both of which show that though wicked men persecute the
righteous, God defends and protects them. Both come from the
Greek version of the book of Daniel. The first is that of Daniel, cast
into the lion's den (Dan. 6:16). The second is that of Ananias,
Azariah, and Mishael in the fiery furnace (Dan. 3:19-21). Clement
may have in mind Hellenistic Jewish ideas about those who "fear
God" and worship "the Most High" (see Knopf p. 121; more re-
cently, E. R. Goodenough in *Jewish Quarterly Review* 47 [1957],
221-244); but it is at least equally likely that he takes the epithet

and blameless intent, not knowing that the Most High is the
champion and defender of such as with a clear conscience serve
his most virtuous name; to whom be glory for ever and ever.
Amen. 8. But those who endured with confidence inherited glory
and honor, were exalted and inscribed by God on his memory
for ever and ever. Amen.

46 We too, brethren, must follow such examples as these. 2.
For it is written, "Cling to the saints, for those who cling to them
will be sanctified" [source unknown]. 3. And again, in another
place it says, "With the innocent man you will be innocent and
with the chosen you will be chosen and with a perverse man
you will deal perversely" [Ps. 17:26-27]. 4. Let us then imitate
the innocent and righteous, for such are the chosen of God. 5.
Why is there strife and passion and dissension and schism and

---

"Most High" from the Old Testament (as in his quotations in 29:2
and 52:3), especially from the book of Daniel itself (2:19; 3:26).
His mention of the sequence Ananias, Azariah, and Mishael strongly
suggests that he is using the longer (LXX) version of Daniel (3:24);
compare Origen, *De oratione* 13, 2 (p. 326, 24 Koetschau) and,
especially, *Ep. ad Africanum* 2 (PG 11, 52A). For further use of
"apocrypha" by Clement see 55:4-6.

The concluding phrase (*en tōi mnēmosynōi autou*) is found seventy-
one times in the Septuagint. It expresses the standing hope and plea
that God "remember" Israel (for the significance of this see C. P.
Price, *Remembering and Forgetting in the Old Testament and Its
Bearing on the Early Christian Eucharist* [Ann Arbor, Mich., University Microfilms, 1963], 80-149).

46:1-9. Christians must "cling" (see commentary on 15:1) to the
examples given in 45:3-8; they must obey the scriptural (apocryphal)
saying, "Cling to the saints, for those who cling to them will be
sanctified." This saying seems to be echoed in Hermas, Similitudes 8,
8, 1 and in some manuscripts of Visions 3, 6, 2. Clement reinforces
his counsel with a quotation from Psalm 17:26-27 ("in another
place") and then paraphrases what he has quoted.

Next he passes on to ask a series of three rhetorical questions probably based on New Testament books and reaching a climax when he
refers to "such a degree of madness" in the third. The first resembles
James 4:1; the second contains echoes of Ephesians 4:4-6; and the
third echoes Romans 12:5. All three New Testament passages are
concerned with the unity of the community.

Christians must "remember the words of the Lord Jesus" (cf.
13:1-2). The words are these (very literally translated):

contention among you? 6. Have we not one God and one Christ and one Spirit of grace which was poured out upon us—one calling in Christ? 7. Why do we rend and tear apart the members of Christ and revolt against our own body, and reach such a degree of madness as to forget that we are members one of another? Remember the words of the Lord Jesus, 8. for he said, "Woe to that man; it were better for him that he had not been born than that he should cause one of my elect to stumble. It were better for him that a millstone be hanged about his neck and that he be drowned in the sea, than that he should cause one of my elect to sin" [Matt. 26:24 and parallels, Luke 17:1 and parallels, conflated and paraphrased]. 9. Your schism has caused many to sin, has made many doubt, has made many despair, has brought grief upon all. And still your rebellion goes on!

C. The necessity of love (47:1–50:7)

47 Take up the letter of blessed Paul the apostle. 2. What did he first write to you "in the beginning of the gospel"? [Phil. 4:15.] 3. Truly it was by the Spirit that he wrote you concerning himself and "Cephas and Apollos" [1 Cor. 1:10 ff.], because

Woe to that man;	Matt. 26:24 (Mark 14:21) Luke 22:22
it were good for him not to be born	Matt. 26:24 (Mark 14:21)
rather than to scandalize one of my elect;	
it were better for a millstone to be put on him and	Matt. 18:6 (Mark 9:42) Luke 17:2
for him to be drowned in the sea than to turn aside one of my elect.	Matt. 18:6 (Mark 9:42) Luke 17:2

This passage is certainly not based directly on our written Gospels; instead, as Koester pp. 16–19 has argued, it comes from tradition either oral or written, or, as is also possible, from memory quotation.

Clement concludes with a rhetorical statement on the effects of the schism. Three verbs show its effect on "many"; one indicates the grief of "all"; in spite of these consequences the sedition continues.

47:1–50:7. Clement's use of Pauline expressions (46:6–7) and his mention of "schism" (46:5, 9) prepares the way for direct employment of 1 Corinthians, in which "schism" is a primary theme (1 Cor. 1:10; 11:18). The situation then was more excusable than the shameful one now (ch. 47). The only way to put an end to it is through prayer for mercy and reconciliation to God, so that he will restore

even then you had developed factions. 4. But that partisanship
involved you in less sin, for you were partisans of distinguished
apostles and of a man certified by them. 5. Now, however, think
again, consider who has led you astray and lessened respect for
your far-famed brotherly love. 6. It is disgraceful, beloved,

---

brotherly love in the community "without disturbance"; those who
think they are great must be humble and seek the good of all (ch.
48). The greatest gift of God is *agapē* (ch. 49)—for which Christians
must pray and work (ch. 50).

According to Meinhold pp. 99–108, Clement appeals to 1 Corinthians because the Corinthians are still, or again, "pneumatics";
their emphasis on spiritual gifts is responsible for the schism (see
commentary on ch. 15). This theory is possible, but the objections of
Wrede pp. 34–35 remain convincing: had Clement wanted to say
that they were "pneumatics" he would have done so.

47:1–7. To the Corinthians Clement recalls "the letter of blessed
Paul the apostle." Elsewhere he has spoken of Peter and Paul as "the
good apostles" (5:3) or has simply mentioned "the apostles" (42:1–
2) or "our apostles" (44:1). Beginning with chapter 40, however, he
has tended to apply the epithet "blessed" to various persons—Moses
(43:1) and other liturgical ministers (40:4; 44:5; 48:4). The most
striking feature of his admonition lies in his mention of one epistle,
first written to the Corinthians at "the beginning of the gospel" (an
allusion to Phil. 4:15, which in turn refers to Paul's ministry at
Corinth). Lightfoot pp. 142–143 points out that early Christian
writers sometimes speak of Corinthians, Thessalonians, and Timothy
as if only one letter were written to each (similarly they seem to
combine 1 and 2 John); he claims that "where the context clearly
shows which epistle is meant, no specification is needed," but admits
that there are no clear allusions to 2 Corinthians in Clement's letter
(cf. Knopf pp. 122–123). The theory that Clement is referring to a
collection of Paul's letters headed ("first") by 1 Corinthians is untenable because Clement's word "first" is explained by "the beginning
of the gospel." As Sanders (p. 155, n. 1) observes, "It is rather
unlikely that in these words Clement concealed subtle nuances
destined to be discovered by future historians of the canon."

Paul was inspired by the Spirit (cf. 1 Cor. 7:40) as he wrote about
Corinthian partisanship, for his words are relevant not only to the
past situation but also to the present. Then, however, the Corinthians
were partisans of Paul, Cephas, and Apollos (Paul's own order is
Paul, Apollos, Cephas: 1 Cor. 1:12; 3:22)—two "distinguished" (cf.
17:1) apostles and one man approved by them (cf. 42:4; 44:2;
Apollos evidently is subordinate to the apostles, as in 1 Cor. 16:12).
The fact that Clement does not mention partisans of Christ (1 Cor.
1:12) proves nothing about his text of 1 Corinthians; they are not

utterly disgraceful, and unworthy of Christian conduct, to have
it reported that because of one or two persons the ancient and
well-established Corinthian Church is in revolt against the elders. 7. Furthermore, this report has reached not only us, but also
those who differ with us, so that you heap blasphemies upon the
name of the Lord through your folly and create danger for yourselves as well.

48 Let us put an end to this forthwith, and fall down before
your Master, and implore him with tears to be merciful to us
and to be reconciled to us and to restore us to that worthy and
reverent exercise of brotherly love that befits us. 2. For this is
the gate of righteousness opening into life, as it is written, "Open
to me the gates of righteousness; when I have entered therein I
shall praise the Lord. 3. This is the gate of the Lord, the
righteous shall enter by it" [Ps. 117:19–20]. 4. For many gates
stand open: the gate of righteousness is the gateway of Christ,

---

mentioned in 1 Corinthians 3:22 and, indeed, may not have existed
as a separate group. For another picture of early Christianity at
Corinth see chapters 1–3, from which (1:1) the phrase "venerable
and famous" is repeated.

The Corinthians' current partisanship is much worse than that in
former times, for now it is due to one or two persons, results in revolt, and is known to non-Christians (Knopf p. 124 points out that
Paul too was concerned with this question: 1 Cor. 10:32; 1 Thess.
4:12; add 1 Cor. 5–6). In consequence, they bring blasphemy upon
the name of the Lord (cf. Rom. 2:24; 2 Clem. 13) and danger upon
themselves—the danger of damnation (14:2; 41:4; 59:1; so Lightfoot
p. 145; Knopf p. 124).

48:1–6. The resolution of this problem is to be found in falling
down before God our Master and beseeching him (cf. Heb. 5:7) for
mercy and reconciliation—not so much reconciliation within the community as God's being reconciled with us, which will lead to his
restoring brotherly love (cf. 47:5). Repentance will open "the gates
of righteousness," one of which is "the gate of the Lord" (Ps. 117:19–
20). Of these gates the principal one is that "of Christ." It is possible,
but most uncertain, that Clement has in mind the word of Jacob:
"This is none other than the house of God, and this is the gate of
heaven" (Gen. 28:17; cf. John 1:51); but his thought is not usually
so speculative. He immediately turns to a famous passage in Paul
on Christian unity of the Church (1 Cor. 12:8–9 [cf. also 13:2];
cf. his use of 1 Cor. 12:21–23 in 37:5, and 12:4 in 38:1), where we
find faith, knowledge, and wisdom; purity in action may possibly

and all are blessed who enter by it and direct their way "in
holiness and righteousness" [Luke 1:75], accomplishing all things
without disorder. 5. Let a man be faithful, let him be capable of
uttering knowledge, let him be discriminating in the evaluation
of what is said, let him be pure in conduct. 6. For the greater
he seems to be, the humbler he ought to be, and the more
zealous for the common good rather than his own.

49 Let him who in Christ has love fulfill the commandments
of Christ. 2. The bond of the love of God—who can adequately
describe it? 3. The greatness of its beauty—who is capable of
putting it into words? 4. The height to which love leads us is
beyond description. 5. Love unites us to God, "love covers a
multitude of sins" [1 Pet. 4:8; cf. Jas. 5:20], love bears all things,
is patient in all things. There is nothing vulgar about love,
nothing arrogant. Love knows nothing of schism, love does not

---

come from 2 Corinthians 7:11 (Ziegler p. 55). Greatness involves
humility, interpreted as work for the common good (cf. 37:4–38:2:
also 57:2). See also Mark 10:43–44 and parallels.

49:1–6.   Love, like faith (32:4–33:1), requires expression in works,
in performance of Christ's commands. At this point Clement turns to
a panegyric on *agapē* in which Pauline and more generally Hellenistic
motifs are obviously combined (see A. Nygren, *Agape and Eros*
[London, 1953], 247–249). Love is a "bond" as in Colossians 3:14;
it possesses great beauty; and it lifts us to "the height" (cf. the
followers of Prodicus in Clement, *Str.* 3, 28, 5). According to Nygren
(*op. cit.*, 248), "as a whole, this hymn to Agape exalts love as in-
comparably the greatest human achievement." He bases this judgment
on two points: (1) "love covers a multitude of sins" refers not to
forgiveness of one's neighbor but to "the ability of Agape to win
forgiveness from God," and (2) "man can, by the exercise of his
love, ascend to God." This criticism is in part correct; it neglects,
however, Clement's practical purpose: love contains no schism, does
not revolt, does everything in harmony—all important themes of the
letter and especially of this part of it. Similarly, Paul's account of
love in 1 Corinthians 13 is directly related to his practical purpose.
Neither Paul nor Clement was writing abstractly or even "theo-
logically." Moreover, when Nygren (*op. cit.*, 249, n. 2) quotes
Harnack as saying, "Again the author feels it necessary to mention
the blood of Christ," this remark implies that Clement really did not
want to mention it. Actually, he mentions the blood of Christ as
evidence for God's love. He gave his blood "by the will of God" (cf.
John 6:38–40) "for us" (cf. Luke 22:20), his flesh for our flesh (cf.

rebel, love does all things in harmony; in love all the elect of
God are made perfect, without love nothing is pleasing to God.
6. In love our Master received us; because of the love he had for
us our Lord Jesus Christ by the will of God shed his blood for
us, gave his flesh for our flesh and his life for our lives.

50 You see, brethren, how great and wondrous a thing love is,
and that its perfection is beyond description. 2. Who is able to
be found in it except those whom God considers worthy? Let
us then beg and beseech his mercy that we may be found blameless in love, without human partiality. 3. All the generations from
Adam to our day have passed away, but those made perfect in
love according to the grace of God have a place among the
godly who will be made manifest when Christ's kingdom comes.
4. For it is written, "Enter into your inner rooms for a little

---

John 6:51, "my flesh for the life of the world"), his soul (or life) for
our souls (or lives).

The Old Testament background of Clement's statement is equally
important. It seems to be based directly on exegesis of Leviticus
17:11, where we read that "the soul of all flesh is its blood; and I
have given it for you . . . to make atonement for your souls; for its
blood makes atonement in place of the soul" (LXX). Clement treats
this text in relation to the sacrifice of the blood (7:4; 12:7; 21:6) of
Jesus Christ. He gave his blood "for us"; this means (1) that he gave
his flesh, and (2) that he gave his soul also. A similar passage in
Irenaeus (*Adv. haer.* 5, 1, 1) may well be based on 1 Clement.

50:1–3. Love, as Clement has just shown, is "great and wondrous"
(he uses the phrase in 26:1 in a different sense); its perfection (cf.
1 John 2:5; 4:12, 18) cannot be expressed (cf. 49:4). Actually, it is
a gift of divine grace, and we can only pray for it. It excludes
partisan spirit (21:7; 47:3–4). Even though all the past generations
have passed away, those made perfect in love by God's grace are
waiting in God's "inner rooms" (Isa. 26:20), in "the place among the
godly" (cf. 5:4, 7; perhaps 44:5), for the visitation of the kingdom
of Christ. The "place" is the abode of the righteous dead before
the last judgment; see 1 Enoch 22 and 2 Esdras 7:78–99 (Knopf p.
127). Polycrates of Ephesus (*ca.* 190) describes Melito of Sardis as
buried in Sardis and "awaiting the visitation from the heavens, at
which he will rise from the dead" (Eusebius, *H.E.* 5, 24, 5). Biblical
quotations now prove that the forgiveness of sins is a consequence
of love.

50:4–7. The first quotation ("it is written") is very inexact: Isaiah
26:20 reads, "Enter into thy chambers, close thy door, hide for a

while, until my wrath and anger pass, and I will remember a
good day and I will raise you up from your graves" [Isa. 26:20
abridged; Ezek. 37:12 for substance of last clause]. 5. Blessed
are we, beloved, if we keep God's commandments in the harmony of love, so that our sin is forgiven through love. 6. For it
is written, "Blessed are those whose iniquities are forgiven, and
whose sins are covered; blessed is the man against whom the
Lord will not reckon his sin" [Rom. 4:7–9; Ps. 31:1–2] and in
whose "mouth there is no guile" [Ps. 31:2b]. 7. This blessedness
comes upon those who were chosen by God through Jesus Christ
our Lord, to whom be glory for ever and ever. Amen.

D. Practical conclusions about obedience (51:1–58:2)

51 So, then, whatever sins we have committed, and whatever
we have done through the promptings of the adversary, let us
ask that they be forgiven us; and those who have become the

---

little while until the wrath of the Lord passes away," while the end
of the quotation comes from Ezekiel 37:12, "I will lead you forth
from your graves." Perhaps Clement is quoting from an apocryphal
Ezekiel used by other Christians (see the references in the commentary on ch. 8).

It is clear that to be manifest when Christ's kingdom comes involves resurrection (see chs. 23–27). Those who are made perfect in
love (cf. 49:5) are those who obey God's commandments in "the
harmony of love" and thereby have their sins forgiven. Clement must
have in mind the statement that "love covers a multitude of sins" (1
Pet. 4:8, etc.) which he has quoted in 49:5, for he immediately provides another Old Testament quotation which deals with the cover-
ing of sins but not with love. Part of this quotation, which comes
from Psalm 31:1–2, is also found in Romans 4:7–8 (where love is
not discussed); and Clement apparently has Romans in mind, since
he continues with the expression "this blessedness" found in Romans
4:9 (Knopf p. 128), and what he says about the blessing summarizes
what Paul says in the rest of Romans 4: it was given to those chosen
by God through Jesus Christ our Lord. The chapter ends with a
brief doxology, which also terminates this section of the letter.

Actually, the Old Testament quotations do not seem very well
suited for Clement's argument and they contain no reference to the
Christian love of which he is speaking. It is possible that at this point
he is making use of an anthology of Old Testament texts, already put
together in reference to the forgiveness of sins; compare the texts
quoted in chapters 51–52, and the introduction.

51:1–58:2. At this point, following his discussion of brotherly

leaders of revolt and dissension ought to reflect upon the hope
we have in common. 2. Surely those who lead a life of godly
fear and love would rather suffer tortures themselves than have
their neighbors do so, and would rather bear condemnation
themselves than have it fall upon the harmony well and up-
rightly handed down to us. 3. Surely it is well for man to confess

---

love (*philadelphia*, chs. 47–48) and love in general (chs. 49–50),
Clement turns to give specific counsel to the Corinthian dissenters.
His counsel consists not of chapters 51–55 (Klevinghaus pp. 55–57)
but of chapters 51–58 (Knopf p. 128). In chapters 51–53 Old Testament texts prove that God punishes men whose hearts are hardened
(ch. 51) but forgives those who confess (ch. 52); Moses asked forgiveness for all or obliteration with all (ch. 53). The Corinthian leaders should imitate Moses (ch. 54) by voluntarily exiling themselves
—like pagan rulers, other Christians, and women in the Old Testament, all of whom sacrificed themselves for others (ch. 55). Such
chastisement (*paideia*, not in the sense of education or culture) is
from God (ch. 56); therefore the leaders must submit to God—as
Wisdom says in Proverbs (ch. 57), obey him and receive the counsel of the Roman church (ch. 58).

51:1–2. Chapter 50 brought the previous section to an end with
consideration of the blessings of love, along with an exhortation to
pray for it (50:2). Now Clement begins his new section, addressed
primarily to the "leaders of revolt," with an exhortation to pray for
forgiveness of transgressions due to yielding to "the adversary" (Satan,
mentioned only here; in 3:4 Clement apparently omits a reference to
the devil from Wisd. 2:24). For the appellation see 1 Timothy 5:14–
15. The leaders (cf. Heb. 2:10, Christ as "leader" of salvation) of
revolt or sedition (frequent in Clement; see commentary on ch. 63)
and division (46:5; cf. 20:4) must consider Christian fellowship in
hope (cf. 11:1; 12:7; 27:1), which involves suffering tortures (like
the martyrs of 6:1; cf. 45:7) and condemnation for oneself rather
than having one's neighbors suffer (cf. 2:6; 38:1) or bringing discredit upon the traditional Christian unison. This is what living in
community (*politeuomenoi*, see commentary on 1:1) involves—living
with fear of God (2:8; 3:4; 21:6–8; 22:1; 57:5) and love of neighbor (chs. 49–50). The theme of suffering loss rather than harming
one's neighbor is Pauline; compare 1 Corinthians 6:7–8; also the
"words of the Lord Jesus" in 13:2.

51:3–5. Confession (cf. 52:1; 61:3; and in citations 26:2; 48:2;
52:2) is better than hardness of heart like that of the rebels against
"God's servant Moses" (cf. 4:12; 17:5; 43:1)—for their hardness see
Numbers 16:26 LXX (Wrede p. 63). With words taken from Numbers 16:33 ("they went down into Hades alive") Clement combines
a phrase from Psalm 48:14: "death will be [is] their shepherd." As

his sins rather than harden his heart as the hearts of those were
hardened who rebelled against Moses the servant of God, whose
condemnation was made evident. 4. For "they went down into
Hades alive" and "death was their shepherd" [Num. 16:30–33;
Ps. 48:15]. 5. Pharaoh and his army and the rulers of Egypt, "the
chariots and their riders" [Exod. 14:23] were engulfed in the
sea for no other reason than that they hardened their foolish
hearts after signs and wonders were done in Egypt through
God's servant Moses.

52   The Master, brethren, has no need of anything; he wants
nothing of anyone save that he should praise him. 2. As his
chosen one, David, says, "I will praise the Lord [Ps. 7:18] and
this will please him more than a young calf with horns and
hoofs; let the poor see it and rejoice" [Ps. 68:31–33 abridged].
3. And again he says, "Offer to God the sacrifice of praise and
pay your vows to the Most High; call upon me in the day of

Wrede p. 62 points out, the preceding phrase in the psalm is this:
"like sheep they were placed in Hades"; and this fact suggests that
Clement is quoting from memory. Another instance of hardhearted-
ness is that of Pharaoh and the other Egyptians (cf. Exod. 14:17),
"the chariots and their riders" (Exod. 14:23, 26, 28); they perished
because their "unintelligent hearts" (cf. Rom. 1:21; also 36:2) were
hardened—in spite of "signs and wonders" (cf. Exod. 7:3–4; Rom.
9:17–18). Clement regards hardness of heart as a human sin, not
(as in Exodus and Romans) as the consequence of divine predestination. This is because (like Paul in 1 Cor. 10:6–10) he is addressing
members of the Christian community, not explaining the sin of outsiders.

52:1–4.   For a selection of passages to show that the Corinthian
leaders must repent (cf. chs. 7–8) and confess to God, Clement
turns, it would appear, to an anthology originally compiled for quite
another purpose, namely, against sacrifices. The Master needs
nothing (cf. Acts 17:25 and the other passages cited by Knopf p.
129) but confession. Therefore Clement quotes Psalm 7:18 plus
Psalm 68:31–33, Psalm 49:14–15, and Psalm 50:19. A similar anthology is reflected in Barnabas 2:4–10, where Psalm 50:19 (from a
somewhat different text) is also quoted. On such anthologies in the
early Church cf. P. Prigent, *L'épître de Barnabé I-XVI et ses sources*
(Paris, 1961); A. Benoit in *Texte und Untersuchungen* 79 (1961),
20–27; J.-P. Audet in *Revue biblique* 70 (1963), 381–405.

For "the sacrifice of praise" in another context see 35:12 (Ps.
49:16–23).

your affliction and I will deliver you, and you will glorify me"
[Ps. 49:14–15]. 4. For "the sacrifice of God is a broken spirit"
[Ps. 50:19].

53 Now, you know the holy scriptures, beloved, you know
them well, and you have studied the oracles of God, so it is only
to remind you that we write as we do. 2. As you know, when
Moses went up into the mountain and spent forty days and
forty nights in fasting and humiliation, God said to him, "Go
down quickly from here, for your people whom you led out of
Egypt have broken the law; they have quickly turned aside from
the way which you commanded them; they have made for themselves idols." 3. And the Lord said to him, "I have spoken to you
once and again to say, I have seen this people, and behold, it is
stiff-necked: let me destroy them, and I will wipe out their name
from under the heavens, and I will make of you a nation great
and wonderful and far more numerous than they" [Deut. 9:12–

53:1–5. As in 45:2 and 62:3, Clement praises his readers for their
diligent study of the Old Testament scriptures and oracles. For the
emphatic repetition of the verb compare 47:6: "It is disgraceful, . . .
utterly disgraceful" (Knopf p. 130). He is simply reminding them
of what they ought to know; compare 13:1 and 46:7, also 1
Corinthians 11:2. After Moses had spent forty days and nights (Exod.
34:28; Deut. 9:9) in fasting and humiliation (cf. Esther in 55:6),
God spoke to him—and there follows an exact quotation from
Deuteronomy 9:12–14 (except that, as in Barn. 4:8 and 14:3, Clement adds the words, "Moses, Moses," doubtless reflecting a Septuagint
text used by early Christians). For Moses' reply he turns to the
parallel account in Exodus 32:31–32. For "I beseech thee" in Exodus
he substitutes "by no means" in order to emphasize Moses' boldness;
for "thy book which thou didst write" he substitutes "the book of
the living." This book (plural in Hermas, Sim. 2, 9) is mentioned in
Psalm 68:29: "Let them be blotted out of the book of the living,"
and in the first-century Palestinian recension of the twelfth of the
Eighteen Benedictions—where it has a particular reference to Jewish
Christians (cf. W. D. Davies, *The Setting of the Sermon on the
Mount* [Cambridge, 1964], 275–276). If Clement knew this Benediction—as is not impossible—he was probably influenced more by
its phrasing than by its thought, although in chapter 54 he passes on
to something not unlike excommunication, or at least self-excom-
munication (note that the word "congregation," 53:5, is picked up
in 54:2). The chapter ends with a rhetorical flourish which recalls
the thoughts of 50:1.

14; Exod. 32:7–10]. 4. And Moses said, "By no means, Lord! Pardon the sin of this people, or else wipe me also out of the book of the living" [Exod. 32:32]. 5. What great love! What unsurpassable perfection! The servant addresses his Lord boldly, to ask of him forgiveness for the whole congregation.

54 Among you, then—who is noble, who is compassionate, who is really loving? 2. Let him say, "If it is because of me that rebellion and strife and schism have arisen, I will leave, I will go wherever you wish, I will do whatever the congregation commands. Only let the flock of Christ live at peace with its appointed elders." 3. The man who does this will win for himself great fame in Christ, and will be welcome everywhere. For "the earth is the Lord's and the fullness thereof" [Ps. 23:1]. 4. This

---

54:1–4. This is one of the most important chapters in the letter, for between two collections of examples Clement inserts a direct appeal to the leaders of the revolt (cf. 51:1) at Corinth. He first suggests that among them there may be someone noble (like the apostles, 5:1; like Paul's fame, 5:6; like the Roman Christians' prize, 6:2—or even like the phoenix, 25:3!), compassionate (like God, 29:1), and filled with love (chs. 49–50). Then he urges such a person to admit his responsibility for the revolt (mentioned nine times in the letter), strife (also nine times), and divisions (five times singular or plural), and to enter upon voluntary exile. This theme is common among Greek and Roman rhetoricians (Sanders pp. 42–47, 52–55) but Clement develops it in a special way. The exile is to go wherever Clement chooses and will do what "the congregation" (Clement thus speaks in the name of the whole Christian Church, a community comparable to Israel) commands. The exile's only goal is to be peace for "the flock of Christ" (cf. 44:3 and commentary)—with the presbyters set over it (cf. 44:5; 57:1–2).

Under such circumstances the exile will acquire "great fame in Christ" (i.e., in the churches; cf. 2 Cor. 8:18) and will be received everywhere, presumably with Clement's commendation. Psalm 23:1 shows that the whole earth is the Lord's; the Christian exile will be received everywhere because he has done the Lord's work, and is commended by those who do it.

Those who live as citizens of God's state have acted in this way (Moses, 53:4–5; Judith and Esther, 55:4–6; other Christians, 55:2) and will do so again. On Christianity as a *politeia* see 2:8; 3:4; 6:1; 21:1; 44:6; 51:1.

For contemporary interest in exile see Plutarch's treatise *De exilio*.

has been and always will be the practice of those who follow God's way of life, that brings no regrets.

55 To take some heathen examples as well: In times of plague, many kings and rulers, in response to an oracle, have given themselves up to death in order that their people might be rescued through their blood. Many have left their own cities, lest their revolt go farther. 2. We know of many among us who have delivered themselves to bondage in order to ransom others; many have sold themselves into slavery and used the price paid for themselves to feed others. 3. Many women have been enabled by the grace of God to perform deeds worthy of heroic men. 4. The blessed Judith, when her city was besieged, begged of the elders that she be permitted to go out into the enemy encampment. 5. Though exposing herself to danger, she went out

---

55:1–6. After the appeal for voluntary exile in chapter 54, Clement supplies seven examples or models, first from the Gentiles, then from Christians, and finally from Jewish women. He begins with "many" cases (vss. 1–3) and then supplies specific names (vss. 4–6; cf. Ziegler p. 98).

55:1 consists of a general statement or rhetorical topic; its theme is *dulce et decorum est pro patria mori* (cf. Cicero, *Tusculanae Disputationes* 1, 116; Knopf p. 132; Sanders pp. 42–47). In addition, he supplies details (kings and rulers, calamity, oracles, the sacrifice of blood) which are characteristic of the way in which the theme was handled (Sanders pp. 52–55; oracles are probably not significantly Corinthian, against Ziegler pp. 60–73).

55:2–6 is oddly reminiscent of 1 Corinthians 13:3 (ch. 13 is used in 1 Clem. 49:5).

Many among us *delivered* themselves to bonds in order to ransom others (cf. 55:1);	If I *deliver* my body . . .
many delivered themselves to slavery and with the price *fed* others.	if I *feed* [men with] all my possessions . . .

Compare also 1 Corinthians 9:19: "Though free from all I enslaved myself to all in order to gain more." The parallels make an enigmatic passage more enigmatic; but it seems clear that, however he phrases it, Clement is giving facts about the Roman community and its Christian actions (see Ignatius, Rom. 2:2). Finally, by grace the weak are made strong (cf. 2 Cor. 12:9) and women exhibit manliness (*andreia*). Clement's examples come from the Greek Old Testament. First he mentions the "blessed" Judith (his is the first reference to

for love of country and of her besieged people, and the Lord
delivered Holofernes into a woman's hand [Judith 8–13]. 6. Like-
wise Esther, perfect in faith, exposed herself to no less danger,
in order to deliver the twelve tribes of Israel from the brink of
destruction; for by her fasting and self-humiliation she implored
the all-seeing Master [cf. Esther 15:5 LXX], the eternal God, and
he, when he saw the humility of her soul, delivered the people
for whose sake she had endangered herself [Esther 7–9].

56 We too then must intercede for those who have fallen into
any sin, so that forbearance and humility may be given them to

---

the book) but does not linger over the details of how she beheaded
Holofernes. The expression "into a woman's hand" comes from
Judith 13:15 or 16:6. Next he speaks of Esther, obviously relying on
the Septuagint, since in the Hebrew text God is not mentioned.
Esther's fasting (Esther 4:16) and humiliation (4:8) preceded her
invocation of the all-seeing God (15:5). For the emphasis on women's
virtues compare the contemporary work by Plutarch, *De virtutibus
mulierum*.

It should be noted that, as in Esther, fasting and humiliation (humility) are two different things; this confirms the view of W. C. van
Unnik (*Zeitschrift für die neutestamentliche Wissenschaft* 44 [1952–
53], 250–255) that *tapeinophrosyne* and similar words are not to be
translated as "fasting."

Since Clement's references are important for the history of the Old
Testament in the Church (for his version of Daniel see commentary
on ch. 45), we should say something about the evidence roughly contemporary with his. (1) Judith is mentioned as one of "the saints" by
Tertullian, *De monogamia* 17, 1; and while Clement of Alexandria's
mention of her in *Stromata* 4, 118, 4 comes from 1 Clement, he independently alludes to Judith 8:27 in *Stromata* 2, 35, 4. In Origen's
time Palestinian Jews did not use the book even "among the apocrypha
(hidden books)" (*Ep. ad Africanum* 13; PG 11, 80B), but he himself uses it fairly frequently: *Str.* 6 frag. (PG 11, 102A); *Ioh.
comm.* 2, 22 (p. 78, 33 Preuschen); *Iudic. hom.* 9, 1 (p. 518, 8
Baehrens); *De oratione* 13, 2 (p. 326, 22 Koetschau) and 29, 3 (p.
382, 24). (2) The additions to Esther are clearly attested by Josephus
(*Ant.* 11, 184–296) and alluded to by Clement of Alexandria (*Paed.*
3, 12, 5; *Str.* 4, 119, 1–2, only partly from 1 Clement). Origen
points out that they are not accepted by Jews (*Ep. ad Africanum* 3;
PG 11, 53A) but twice refers to them himself (*De oratione* 13, 2,
p. 326, 19 Koetschau; 14, 3, p. 331, 23).

56:1–16. Because Clement has been insisting so vigorously on the
necessity of obedience and humility, he feels it necessary to remind

submit themselves not to us, but to the will of God. For in that way the merciful remembrance of them in the presence of God and the saints will be fruitful and perfect. 2. Let us accept that discipline which no one should resent, brethren. The reproof which we address to each other is good and entirely beneficial, for it binds us to God's will. 3. For so speaks the holy Word, "The Lord has chastened me sorely, but he has not given me over to death" [Ps. 117:18]. 4. "For the Lord disciplines him whom he loves, and chastises every son whom he receives" [Heb. 12:6; Prov. 3:12]. 5. For it says, "A righteous man will discipline me with mercy and reprove me, but let not the oil of sinners anoint my head" [Ps. 140:5]. 6. And again it says, "Blessed is the man whom the Lord reproves; do not refuse warning from the Almighty. For he inflicts pain, and again he restores. 7. He smites, but his hands heal. 8. Six times will he rescue you from distress, and the seventh time evil will not touch you. 9. In famine he will rescue you from death, and in battle he will deliver you from the power of the sword. 10. And from the scourge of the tongue he will hide you, and you will in no way fear the coming evils. 11. You will ridicule the evil

---

his readers that the obedience involved is not in relation to him or the Roman community, but to God's will. He therefore urges that intercessory prayer be offered for the dissidents so that they may have "fruitful and perfect" (cf. 44:5) remembrance before God. He also proceeds to prove from "the holy Word" (cf. 13:3) that mutual admonition (cf. 1 Cor. 4:14) unites Christians to God's will. "Chastening," as Knopf pp. 133–134 points out, is the key word to which the passages quoted from the Old Testament refer: the first three include the verb *paideuō* (Ps. 117:18; Prov. 3:12; Ps. 140:5), while the fourth (Job 5:17–26) lacks the word but includes "admonition" (*nouthetēma*). God's chastening is obviously educational in scope; Clement compares it with that given by "a good father"; but he does not have in mind "an act of Christian education" (in spite of Jaeger pp. 24–26).

Jaeger p. 117 points to passages about *paideia* as showing that Clement had a definite idea about Christian culture as analogous to Greek. He admits that "in the passages in chapter 56 that are taken from the Old Testament, *paideia* has the limited meaning of the Hebrew term for chastisement"—as in Clement's own usage, 56:2, 16, and 57:1. It is true that in 59:3 *epaideusas* means "taught" and in 62:3 Clement speaks of "the oracles of the teaching of God." But this is not enough to show that Clement had a conception of Christian *paideia*; see C. W. Mackauer in *Journal of Religion* 43 (1963), 157.

and the lawless, 12. and the wild beasts shall leave you in peace. 13. Then you will know that your house will be in peace, and the dwelling place of your tent will not be in want. 14. And you will know that your posterity will be numerous, and your children like the abundance of the fields. 15. You will go to your grave like ripe wheat gathered at harvest time, or like a heap on the threshing floor gathered at the right time" [Job 5:17–26]. 16. You see, brethren, what protection is afforded those who are disciplined by the Master; for he is the good Father who disciplines us so that through his holy discipline we may obtain mercy.

57 Hence you who are the instigators of the revolt must submit to the elders and accept discipline in repentance, bending the knees of your hearts. 2. Learn obedience, laying aside the arrogance and proud willfulness of your tongue. For it is better for you to find a small but creditable place in the flock of Christ than to appear eminent but be excluded from his hope. 3. For thus says the excellent Wisdom, "Behold, I will declare to you the utterance of my spirit, and I will teach you my word. 4. Since I called and you did not listen, poured out words and you did

---

57:1–7. The practical solution for the Corinthian problem is therefore to be found either in the voluntary exile of those who created it (chs. 54–55) or in their obedience to the presbyters (54:2) and repentance (chs. 51–52). It is better to be "small" (37:4) in Christ's flock (16:1; 44:3; 54:2) than to be cast out from the common hope (51:1). Dwelling "in hope confidently" (57:7), indeed, seems to be identified as "dwelling with confidence in the Name" of God (58:1).

Clement confirms the truth of what he has said by quoting the words of "excellent (a favorite word; cf. 1:2; 2:3; 45:7; 60:4) Wisdom" from Proverbs 1:23–33. It has sometimes been thought, as by Eusebius (*H.E.* 4, 22, 9), that Hegesippus, Irenaeus, and "the whole chorus of the ancients" (Christians) called Proverbs by the name Wisdom. If this is so, though there is no evidence from Irenaeus to substantiate it, we might suppose that Irenaeus and Hegesippus, both of whom knew 1 Clement, misunderstood this passage—where Clement clearly is identifying the speaker in his text of Proverbs. In 58:1 he refers to "the threats uttered by Wisdom." Elsewhere in the letter "wisdom" is an attribute either of God (18:6) or of men (13:1; 32:4; 38:2; 39:6).

not heed, but disregarded my counsels and disobeyed my admonitions, therefore I will laugh at your destruction and I will rejoice when ruin comes upon you and when confusion suddenly overtakes you, and catastrophe descends like a whirlwind, or when persecution and siege come upon you. 5. For it shall be that when you call upon me, I will not listen to you; the wicked shall seek me, and will not find me. For they hated wisdom, and rejected the fear of the Lord, nor were they willing to heed my counsels but mocked my reproofs. 6. For this reason they will eat the fruits of their own conduct and be filled with their own godlessness. 7. Because they wronged babes they shall be killed, and a searching inquiry will destroy the godless. But he that listens to me will dwell in hope confidently and will live quietly, free from all fear of evil" [Prov. 1:23–33].

58 Let us then obey his most holy and glorious Name and escape the threats against the disobedient uttered long ago by Wisdom, that we may dwell with confidence in his most holy and exalted Name. 2. Follow our advice and you will not regret it. For as God lives, and the Lord Jesus Christ lives, and the Holy Spirit, the object of faith and hope for the elect, the man who with humility and eager gentleness obeys without regret the righteous commandments of God, this man will be listed and enrolled in the number of those who are saved through Jesus Christ, through whom be glory to God for ever and ever. Amen.

58:1–2. In view of the threats expressed by God's Wisdom (57:3) we must obey God's "most holy and glorious Name" and "dwell with confidence" (from 57:7) in "his most holy and exalted Name." On God's Name see commentary on chapter 64. Clement then promises that if the Corinthian rebels take his advice they will have no regrets; he confirms the promise by a solemn oath which in form resembles that taken by God in 8:2 (Ezek. 33:11) and in content is threefold, and therefore proleptically Trinitarian. The three persons are God, the Lord Jesus Christ, and the Holy Spirit (the faith and hope of the elect); compare "one God and one Christ and one Spirit of grace which was poured out upon us" (46:6). The Corinthians—if they obey God's commandments—will be enrolled and indeed illustrious among the number (cf. 2:4; 35:4; 59:2) of those being saved (for the language cf. Acts 2:47; 4:4; 6:7). The chapter ends with a brief doxology.

E. Solemn liturgical conclusion (59:1–61:3)

59 If on the other hand there are some who disobey what is told them by him through us, let them know that they involve themselves in sin and no small peril. 2. But we shall be guiltless of this sin and we shall beg with earnest prayer and supplication that the Creator of all things will keep intact the precise number of his elect in all the world through his beloved Servant Jesus Christ, through whom he has called us from darkness into light,

---

59:1–61:3. Those who disobey the words of this letter will be disobeying God (59:1), but Clement himself will pray for the security of the elect (59:2). This prayer begins with a statement of God's saving omnipotence (59:3) and an appeal for his succor (59:4). Another statement of his eternal beneficence (60:1) is followed by a petition for mercy (60:2–3), which passes into an appeal for concord and peace (60:4). Intimations of concern for rulers are then developed into a definite intercession on their behalf, for our subjection to them and for their godly administration. The prayer ends with a doxology (ch. 61).

59:1–4. Disobedience to what Clement has said is disobedience toward God, for it is he who has spoken these words (cf. 63:2, "through the Holy Spirit"); it will involve men in danger (14:2). Clement and those with him will be innocent, for they have given sufficient warning and continue to pray for the Creator (20:11; 26:1; 33:2; 35:3) to preserve the number of the elect (cf. 2:4; 46:4; 49:5; 58:2; cf. 1:1; 6:1; 50:7). The title "beloved Servant" (*pais*) for Jesus—only in this chapter of 1 Clement—is characteristic of early Christian prayers (Acts 3:13, 26; 4:27, 30; Did. 9:2–3; 10, 1; Mart. Polyc. 14:1, 3; Hippolytus, *Apostolic Tradition* 3–4) and clearly shows that Clement is about to set forth a solemn prayer; it does not, however, indicate that he is reproducing the Roman liturgy except in so far as he himself was responsible for it. God's calling Christians "from darkness into light" recalls Acts 26:18 (cf. 2 Clem. 1:4–6), and the end of the sentence reminds us of 2 Corinthians 4:6: "The God who said, Out of darkness light shall shine, is he who shone in our hearts for illumination with the knowledge of the glory of God in the person [or, presence] of Christ."

The structure of the sentence is now altered slightly, and God is addressed directly, with the result that some commentators have supposed that a few words have been lost from the text. It is equally possible, however, that as Clement writes he imperceptibly passes from the preface to his prayer into the prayer itself. God "called us . . . to hope in thy Name." The prayer is both universal in content and particular in its application to the Corinthians' circumstances.

from ignorance into the knowledge of the glory of his Name,
3. to hope in thy Name as in the source of all creation.
Thou hast opened the eyes of our hearts to recognize that
thou alone art highest among the highest,
ever remaining holy among the holy.
Thou dost humble the pride of the arrogant,
overthrow the calculations of the nations,
raise up the humble and
humble the proud;
thou dost make rich and make poor,
kill and make alive;
thou alone art the benefactor of spirits and
the God of all flesh.
Thou seest into the depths and lookest upon men's deeds;
thou are the aid of those in peril, Savior of those in despair,
the Creator of every spirit and the Watcher over it.
Thou dost multiply the nations upon the earth and
from them all thou hast chosen those who love thee
through Jesus Christ thy beloved Servant,
through whom thou dost discipline, sanctify, and honor us.
4. We beseech thee, Master, to be our helper and defender.
Save those of us in affliction,
have mercy on the humble,
raise up the fallen,
show thyself to those in need,
heal the sick,
turn back those of thy people who have gone astray.
Feed the hungry,
release our imprisoned ones,

Almost everything in the prayer is based upon Old Testament
language (from the LXX, including the book of Judith, to which
Clement has already referred). For complete references see the
commentaries of Lightfoot and Knopf and the edition of Bihlmeyer–
Schneemelcher. The structure of the prayer (which does not end
before 61:3) in chapter 59 is as follows: (1) Supplication for knowledge of God (59:3a); (2) Ascription of antithetical actions to God
(59:3b); (3) Ascription of providential care to God (59:3c), culminating with our instruction, sanctification, and honor through Jesus
Christ; and (4) Petition for salvation and for knowledge of God and
Jesus Christ (59:4).

revive the weak,
encourage the fainthearted.

Let all the heathen know that thou art God alone, and that
Jesus Christ is thy Servant, and that we are thy people and
the sheep of thy pasture.

60 For thou through thy works didst reveal the everlasting
structure of the universe;
thou, Lord, didst create the world.

Thou art faithful in all generations,
righteous in judgment,
marvelous in might and majesty,
wise in creating,
understanding in establishing what exists,
good toward what is visible, and
kind to those who put their trust in thee,
merciful and compassionate.

Forgive us our lawlessness and unrighteousness,
our transgressions and faults.

2. Reckon not every sin of thy slaves and maidservants, but
cleanse us with the cleansing of thy truth, and guide
our steps

60:1–4. The portion of the prayer included in this chapter begins
with an ascription of praise to God for his work of creation and a
sevenfold statement about his beneficence, which leads into petition
to him as "merciful and compassionate" (a phrase often found in the
Old Testament; cf. Knopf p. 144) to forgive sins both more important
and less important. The petition continues with the prayer that we
may do what is "good and pleasing" before God (cf. 21:1; 35:5)—
and before our rulers, both those of the state (60:4–61:2) and
those of the Church. May we be delivered from sin and from those
who "hate us without a cause" (cf. Ps. 37:19; Justin, *Apology* 1, 14,
3; Knopf p. 145). "Peace," already mentioned in verse 3, becomes
the main theme of the last section. Christians pray for it not only
for themselves but for all who inhabit the earth (a universal note, as
in ch. 20). It is a divine gift formerly given to "our fathers" (cf. 30:7;
62:2) because they called upon God. It is also plainly correlated with
obedience (1) to God's Name, that is, his person and presence (cf.
59:3) and (2) to "our rulers and governors upon earth." The word
"our" is omitted in the Latin version; for its tendentious character at
this point see The Manuscripts and Early Versions, page 4.

that we may walk in holiness of heart and do what is good
and pleasing before thee and before our rulers.

3. Yea, Lord, let thy face shine upon us in peace for our good,
that we may be shielded by thy mighty hand and delivered
from every sin by thy uplifted arm;

and deliver us from those who hate us without a cause.

4. Grant harmony and peace to us and to all who dwell upon
earth,

as thou didst do to our fathers when they reverently called
upon thee in faithfulness and truth;

and grant that we may become obedient to thy almighty and
glorious Name and to our rulers and governors upon
earth.

61 Thou, Master, hast given them the power of sovereignty
through thy excellent and inexpressible might,

so that we may know the glory and honor given them by thee
and be subject to them, in no way resisting thy will:

It is possible, but not certain, that (as C. Taylor, *Sayings of the
Jewish Fathers*, 2d. ed. [Cambridge, 1897], 130 suggested) Clement's
petitions have the Lord's Prayer as their model.

Forgive us . . .	Forgive us our trespasses
Cleanse us . . .	(Marcion reads, "Let thy Holy Spirit . . . cleanse us")
Guide our steps . . .	Lead us not into temptation
Delivered from sin	
Deliver us from those who hate us	Deliver us from evil (or, the evil one)

If we admit this possibility, then we should go on with the doxology
in Matthew, analogous to "the power of sovereignty" in 61:1.

61:1–3. The theme initiated in chapter 60—to please God is to
please our rulers and obedience is due to God and earthly rulers
alike—is now developed more fully. (1) Temporal sovereignty comes
from God and resistance to it is resistance to God's will. (2) Therefore Christians pray for the health, peace, harmony, and stability of
earthly rulers, since this is necessary for their administration. (3) God,
the heavenly master and "King of the ages" (a Jewish expression, cf.
Tobit 13:6, 10; 1 Tim. 1:17), has given "the sons of men glory and
honor" (clearly an allusion to Ps. 8:5–6, taken—as not in Heb. 2:9—
in reference to man in general) and power (Gen. 1:28); therefore
they should administer this power in accordance with what is good
and pleasing before God, that is, religiously, peaceably, and gently.

to them, O Lord, give health, peace, concord, and stability,
that they may administer without offense the governance
thou hast given them.

2. For thou, Master, heavenly King of the ages,
dost give the sons of men glory and honor and power over
what is on earth:
do thou, Lord, direct their will according to what is good
and pleasing before thee,
so that with piety in peace and gentleness they may administer the power given them by thee and may find thee
propitious.

3. To thee, who art alone able to do these things, and more
abundant good things for us,
we offer praise through Jesus Christ,
the High Priest and Guardian of our souls,
through whom be glory and majesty
to thee both now and to all generations,
for ever and ever. Amen.

IV. The Church of Rome and the Church of Corinth (62:1–65:2)

62 We have written enough to you, men and brethren, concerning what befits our religion and what is most particularly

---

Lightfoot p. 179 says that the theme is "in accordance with the
Apostolic injunctions"; Knopf pp. 146–147 gives parallels from second-
century Christian writings. It is more important to note that Clement
goes well beyond anything in the New Testament and prepares the
way for later Christian ideas, although in John 19:11 we read that
Pilate's authority has been given "from above."

Possibly, but by no means certainly, Clement's idea of *exousia* as
given the sons of men is based on something like Matthew 9:8,
where the *exousia* of the Son of man (9:2) is interpreted as given to
men. If he knew something like this it would explain how he could
move from "Son of man" to "man" (cf. again Ps. 8:5).

The prayer ends with a doxology to God through "the High Priest
and Guardian of our souls" (cf. 36:1) and an ascription to him of
"glory and majesty" (20:12). In essence, this doxology is repeated at
the end of chapter 64 and in 65:2.

62:1–65:2. Clement now brings his letter to an end, after the
climactic prayer of chapters 59–61. First he summarizes the nature

helpful to those who intend to lead a virtuous life in reverence
and righteousness. 2. For we have touched upon every topic—
faith, repentance, genuine love, self-control, sound judgment, and
patience, reminding you that we must reverently please almighty
God in righteousness and truth and long-suffering, living in
harmony, without malice, in love and peace, with constant forbearance as did our forefathers mentioned above who pleased
him by their humble attitude toward their God and Father, the
Creator, and toward all men. 3. And we have the more gladly

---

of the "virtuous life" upon which he has laid so much emphasis and
reminds his readers that it is based upon study of the "oracles of
God's teaching" (ch. 62). Next he urges them to respect the great
examples provided from the oracles and to assume the posture of
obedience, rejecting sedition and its source, jealousy, and recovering
peace and concord. He points out that the Roman church has sent
venerable, faithful, and prudent emissaries as witnesses of its care
for peace at Corinth (ch. 63). He adds a benediction upon all the
Corinthians and, indeed, upon all Christians (ch. 64). The letter is
terminated with a request for the speedy return—with good news—
of the Roman emissaries, and with "the grace of our Lord Jesus
Christ" and a final doxology (ch. 65).

62:1–3. As Clement indicates, this is a summary of the contents
of the letter. He has dealt with the Christian religion (thrēskeia) and
especially with its ethical aspects. In so doing he has discussed every
aspect of six virtues which recall the "fruit of the Spirit" in Galatians
5:22–23 (see also ch. 64) and he has reminded the Corinthians (because originally they did obey God; chs. 1–2) that they must please
God in righteousness and truth (cf. 35:2; Eph. 5:9–10) and long-
suffering (Gal. 5:22). They must live in harmony "without malice"
(2:5)—in love and peace (Gal. 5:22) with "eager gentleness" (58:1)
—just as "our fathers" (the Old Testament heroes) pleased God, the
Father and Creator (19:2), and all men as well, by their humility
("eager gentleness" and humility are combined in 58:2; humility is,
of course, the keynote of the letter; see commentary on 13:1–19:1).
Clement adds that he was glad to remind them because he knew that
(like those who appointed the presbyters, 44:2, or the ideal Corinthians, 57:2; 58:2) they were both faithful and distinguished, and
had investigated (40:1; 45:2; 53:1) the oracles of God (13:4; 19:1;
53:1)—or, as Clement puts it more explicitly, "the oracles of the
instruction of God." Jaeger p. 117 rightly paraphrases this expression
as "the sum total of all the Logia of the written tradition" but exag-
gerates somewhat when he speaks of "a new concept of Christian
paideia." Thrēskeia, at the beginning of the chapter, is more important than paideia at the end. In our literature (cf. 45:7) it is most
commonly used in relation to Judaism (Acts 26:5; 4 Macc. 5:7;

reminded you of these things because we knew well that we
were writing to men who are faithful and of good repute and
who have studied the oracles of God's teaching.

63 It is right, therefore, that we should defer to so many examples of such a nature, bow the neck and adopt the attitude
of obedience, so that by giving up this futile rebellion we may
be free of all blame and reach the goal set before us in truth.
2. For you will give us joy and gladness if you prove obedient
to what we have written through the Holy Spirit and desist from
wanton, jealous anger in accordance with the plea for peace and
harmony which we have made in this letter. 3. And we are sending trustworthy and judicious men who from youth to old age
have lived without reproach among us; they will be witnesses
between you and us. 4. We do so in order that you may know
that our whole concern has been and is that you may speedily
be at peace.

64 Finally, may the all-seeing God, the Master of spirits and
Lord of all flesh [Num. 16:22; 27:16; cf. Heb. 12:9] who chose

---

Josephus, *Ant.* 1, 222; 12, 253, 271 [with "ancestral customs"]; *Clem.
hom.* 5, 27). Like Judaism, Christianity was a cult before it was a
philosophy.

63:1–4. Clement has summarized the contents of his letter in
chapter 62; he now indicates what the response of the Corinthians as
a group should be. It is "right" (*themiton*, as Knopf p. 149 points out,
is very rare in early Christian literature) to respect so many (19:1)
examples and to put one's neck (under the yoke and receive instruction
from God's Wisdom, Sir. 51:26) and become obedient, so that by
abandoning sedition (1:1; 2:6; 3:2; 14:2; 46:9; 51:1; 54:2; 57:1)
"we" (Clement means primarily "you") may reach the goal (19:2, of
peace) set before us. The Roman church will be given "joy and
gladness" (messianic in Luke 1:14) if the Corinthians obey what they
have written "through the Holy Spirit" (cf. 59:1) and drive out the
wicked (*athemiton*; contrasted with *themitos* above) wrath due to
jealousy (see chs. 3–4, 6, 9, 14). In this letter Clement has made an
entreaty or "plea" (*enteuxis*) "for peace and harmony"—as he has
repeatedly stated. In addition, the Roman church has sent (three)
representatives (named in 65:1), evidently advanced in years (see
commentary on 1:1), to add their own testimony to what Clement
has written and to report back on the Corinthian situation.

64:1. The final prayer of the letter speaks of the "all-seeing God"

the Lord Jesus Christ and us through him to be his own people
[Deut. 14:2; cf. 7:6; 26:18; Exod. 19:5; Ps. 134:4; Tit. 2:14],
grant to every soul that is called by his exalted and holy Name,
faith, fear, peace, endurance and patience, self-control, purity
and a sound mind, that they may be well pleasing to his Name
through our High Priest and Guardian, Jesus Christ, through
whom to him be glory and majesty, might and honor, both now
and for ever and ever. Amen.

65 Send back to us speedily in peace with joy those sent you
by us, Claudius Ephebus and Valerius Bito, along with Fortunatus, so that they may the sooner report to us the peace and
harmony prayed and longed for, and that we in turn may the
sooner rejoice at your tranquility. 2. The grace of our Lord

(from Esther 15:5 in 1 Clem. 55:6) and describes his universal
dominion in words derived from Numbers 16:22 ("benefactor of
spirits and God of all flesh") and with a reference to God's election
of the Lord Jesus Christ, and through him, of Christians to be "his
own people" (cf. ch. 29). Since those who "are called by his . . .
name" are Christians, the name is presumably "Christ" (cf. Theophilus, *Ad Autol.* 1, 1). Clement prays that Christians may be given
virtues which are essentially the same as the "fruit of the Spirit" in
Galatians 5:22–23 (four sevenths of the list). Clement adds "fear" to
accompany "faith," and "purity and self-control" to expand the notion
of "continence." With these virtues Christians will please God's Name.
   The word "name" in 1 Clement often means no more than "reputation" (1:1) or "title" (43:2; 44:1), but from chapter 43 to the end
of the letter it serves as a way, common also in Judaism, of speaking
of God's person or presence or purpose. Moses acted in order to
glorify God's Name (43:6), which Christians either serve (45:7) or
bring into opprobrium (47:7). This special sense occurs here, as in
58:1 (twice), 59:2 (see commentary), 59:3, and 60:4.
   Christians please God's Name through "our High Priest (cf. 36:1;
61:3; analogous to the Jewish high priest of 40:5 and 41:2) and
guardian (36:1; 61:3) Jesus Christ." A doxology, mostly repeated
from 61:3, concludes the chapter.
   65:1–2. It now becomes clear who the "trustworthy and judicious"
old men are who had been sent by the Roman church to Corinth
(63:3)—they are the messengers Claudius Ephebus and Valerius Bito.
Lightfoot p. 187 points out that such names were fairly common
among slaves or retainers of the Caesars during and after the reign
of Claudius. It is not certain whether or not Fortunatus was one of
the Roman delegates. That he is to be identified with the Fortunatus

Jesus Christ be with you and with all everywhere who have
been called by God through him, through whom to him be
glory, honor, might and majesty, eternal dominion, from everlasting to everlasting. Amen.

---

of 1 Corinthians 16:17—as Lightfoot suggests—is completely uncertain. There is probably a reminiscence of 1 Corinthians 16:11
("send him on in peace") in Clement's instructions to send the messengers back "in peace with joy." The letter proper ends with mention of peace, concord, and good order—its principal themes—and
with a "grace" like those in some of the Pauline epistles; its mention
of "all everywhere" recalls the universalistic emphasis of the preface
to 1 Corinthians (1:2; Lightfoot p. 188). For similar doxological
ascriptions see 61:3; ch. 64; and Revelation 4:11; 5:12, 13. This one
is imitated in the Martyrdom of Polycarp 21.

QUOTATIONS FROM SCRIPTURE

Passage	1 Clement	Introductory Formula
Gen. 1:26–28	33:5–6	thus God spake
Gen. 2:23	6:3	the saying of our father Adam
Gen. 4:3–8	4:1–6	thus it is written
Gen. 12:1–3	10:3	he says to him
Gen. 13:14–16	10:4–5	God said to him
Gen. 15:5–6	10:6	And again it says
Gen. 18:27	17:2	he [Abraham] said
Exod. 2:14	4:10	he [Moses] heard his fellow tribesman say
Exod. 3:11; 4:10	17:5	he [Moses] said
Exod. 32:31–32	53:4	Moses said
Deut. 4:34	29:3	in another place it says
Deut. 9:12–14	53:2–3	God [or the Lord] said to him
Deut. 32:8–9	29:2	thus it is written
Deut. 32:15	3:1	what was written
Ps. 3:6	26:2	and (after a quotation)
Ps. 11:4–5	15:5–6	and again (after a quotation)
Ps. 17:26–27	46:3	in another place it says (after a quotation)
Ps. 18:2–4	27:7	since (no formula)
Ps. 21:7–9	16:15–16	And again he himself [Christ] says (after a quotation)
Ps. 22:4	26:2	(no formula; mixed quotation)
Ps. 23:1	54:3	(no formula)
Ps. 28:7 (?)	26:2	it says somewhere
Ps. 30:19	15:5	(no formula; mixed quotation)
Ps. 31:1–2	50:6	it is written
Ps. 31:10	22:8	(no formula; mixed quotation)
Ps. 33:12–18	22:1–7	Christ himself summons us through the Holy Spirit
Ps. 36:35–37	14:5	And again it says (after a quotation)
Ps. 36:38	14:4	(no formula; mixed quotation)

Passage		1 Clement	Introductory Formula
Ps.	49:14–15	52:3	And again he [David] says
Ps.	49:16–23	35:7	the Scripture says
Ps.	50:3–19	18:2–17	[David] himself says
Ps.	50:19	52:4	(no formula; mixed quotation)
Ps.	61:5	15:3	and again (after a quotation)
Ps.	68:32	52:2	his chosen one, David, says
Ps.	77:36–37	15:4	And again [it says] (after a quotation)
Ps.	88:21	18:1	God said
Ps.	103:4	36:3	thus it is written (from Heb. 1:7)
Ps.	117:18	56:3	so speaks the holy Word
Ps.	117:19–20	48:2–3	as it is written
Ps.	138:7–9	28:3	the Scripture somewhere says
Ps.	140:5	56:5	it [the holy Word] says (after a quotation)
Prov.	1:23–33	57:3	thus says the excellent Wisdom [personified]
Prov.	2:21–22	14:4	it is written
Prov.	3:12	56:4	(no formula; mixed quotation)
Prov.	3:34	30:2	it says
Prov.	20:27	21:2	it says somewhere
Job	1:1	17:3	of Job it is written
Job	4:16–18	39:3–4	it is written
Job	4:19–5:5	39:5–9	(no formula; mixed quotation)
Job	5:17–26	56:6–15	And again it [the holy Word] says
Job	11:2–3	30:4	it says
Job	14:4–5	17:4	he [Job] accuses himself in these words
Job	15:15	39:5	(no formula; mixed quotation)
Job	19:26	26:3	And again Job says
Job	38:11	20:7	he [God] said
Isa.	1:16–20	8:4	in another passage he [the Master] speaks thus
Isa.	6:3	34:6	(no formula; mixed quotation)
Isa.	13:22	23:5	the Scripture . . . says
Isa.	26:20	50:4	it is written
Isa.	29:13	15:2	it says in a certain passage
Isa.	40:10 (?)	34:3	he warns us
Isa.	53:1–12	16:3–14	it [the Holy Spirit] says
Isa.	60:17	42:5	thus says the Scripture somewhere

Passage	1 Clement	Introductory Formula
Isa. 66:2	13:3	the holy Word says
Jer. 9:23–24	13:1	the Holy Spirit says
Ezek. 33:10 (?)	8:2–3	the Master . . . spoke
Dan. 7:10	34:6	the Scripture says
Mal. 3:1	23:5	(no formula; mixed quotation)
unidentified	8:3	adding good advice
	17:6	and again he [it?] says
cf. 2 Clem. 11:2–4	23:3–4	that Scripture . . . which says
cf. Hermas,	46:2	it is written
Sim. 8, 8, 1		

SCRIPTURAL PARAPHRASES AND REFERENCES

Num. 16:30–33	51:3–4
Num. 17	43:2–5
Josh. 2	12:1–8
Esther 7–9	55:6
Judith 8–13	55:4–5

ALLUSIONS TO SCRIPTURE

Passage	1 Clement
Wisd. 2:24	3:4
Wisd. 12:10	7:5
Wisd. 12:12, 11:22	27:5

Summaries and mosaics based on synoptic tradition (cf. H. Koester, *Synoptische Überlieferungen bei den Apostolischen Vätern* [Berlin, 1957])	13:2; 46:8
Possible allusions to the Gospel of John (C. C. Tarelli in *Journal of Theological Studies* 48 [1947], 208–209; M. E. Boismard in *Revue biblique* 55 [1948], 376–387)	42:1–5; 49:1–6
Probable allusions to the Book of Acts (M. Smith in *New Testament Studies* 7 [1960–61], 86–88; also commentary on 37:1)	5:4–6; 37:1, etc.

		1 Clement
Acts	1:3; 2:4; 14:23	42:3–4
Rom.	1:29–32	35:5–6
1 Cor.	1:10 ff.	47:1–3
1 Cor.	1:31 (in O.T. quotation)	13:1
1 Cor.	2:9	34:8
1 Cor.	4:10 (in O.T. quotation)	3:3
1 Cor.	4:14	7:1
1 Cor.	12:4	38:1
1 Cor.	12:8–9	48:5
1 Cor.	12:21–22	37:5
1 Cor.	13:3	55:2
1 Cor.	13:4–7	49:5
1 Cor.	15:20	24:1
1 Cor.	15:23	37:3
1 Cor.	15:35–38	24:5
1 Cor.	16:15	42:4
Gal.	3:1	2:1
Eph.	4:4–6	46:6
Eph.	4:32–5:1	14:3
Eph.	5:21	38:1
Phil.	1:1	42:4
Phil.	4:15	47:2
1 Tim.	1:17	61:2
1 Tim.	2:7	60:4
Titus	3:1	2:7; 33:1; 34:4
Heb.	1:3–5, 7, 13	36:2–5
Heb.	2:17; 3:1	36:1
Heb.	3:2, 5	43:1
Heb.	3:7; 10:15 (formula)	13:1; 16:2 (cf. 8:1; 22:1; 45:2)
Heb.	4:12	21:9
Heb.	4:15	36:1
Heb.	6:18	27:2
Heb. ch. 11 (as a model)		chs. 9–12
Heb.	11:37	17:1
Heb.	12:9	ch. 64
1 Pet.	4:8	49:5

SELECTED BIBLIOGRAPHY

(Books or articles marked * are usually cited only by the author's name)

BARDY, G., "Expressions stoiciennes dans la Iᵃ Clementis," *Recherches de science religieuse* 13 (1922), 73-85.

BOISMARD, M. E., "Clément de Rome et l'Évangile de Jean," *Revue biblique* 55 (1948), 376-387.

CHADWICK, H., "Justification by Faith and Hospitality," *Texte und Untersuchungen* 79 (1961), 281-285.

*EGGENBERGER, C., *Die Quellen der politischen Ethik des 1. Klemensbriefes*. Zurich, 1951.

GIET, S., "Le témoignage de Clément de Rome sur la venue à Rome de Saint Pierre," *Recherches de science religieuse* 29 (1955), 123-136.

HARNACK, A. VON, *Einführung in die alten Kirchengeschichte*. Leipzig, 1929.

*HATCH, E., *Studies in Biblical Greek*. Oxford, 1889.

HEMMER, H., *Clément de Rome*. Paris, 1909.

*JAEGER, W., *Early Christianity and Greek Paideia*. Cambridge, Mass., 1961.

——, "Echo eines unbekannten Tragikerfragments in Clemens' Brief an die Korinther," *Rheinisches Museum* 102 (1959), 330-340.

JAUBERT, A., "Les sources de la conception militaire de l'Église en 1 Clément 37," *Vigiliae Christianae* 18 (1964), 77-84.

*KLEVINGHAUS, J., *Die theologische Stellung der Apostolischen Väter zur alttestamentlichen Offenbarung*. Gütersloh, 1948.

KNOCH, O., "Die Ausführungen des 1. Clemensbriefes über die kirchliche Verfassung im Spiegel der neueren Deutungen seit R. Sohm und A. Harnack," *Theologische Quartalschrift* 141 (1961), 385-407.

*KNOPF, R., *Die Lehre der zwölf Apostel. Zwei Clemensbriefe*. Tübingen, 1920.

*KOESTER, H., *Synoptische Überlieferungen bei den Apostolischen Vätern* (*Texte und Untersuchungen* 65). Berlin, 1957.

LIANG, KWA JOE., *Het begrip Demoed in 1 Clemens*. Utrecht, 1951.

*LIGHTFOOT, J. B., *The Apostolic Fathers, Part I: S. Clement of Rome*. 2 vols. London, 1890. (Citations are from Vol. II.)

*MEINHOLD, P., "Geschehen und Deutung im Ersten Clemensbrief," *Zeitschrift für Kirchengeschichte* 58 (1939), 82-129.

The New Testament in the Apostolic Fathers by a Committee of the Oxford Society of Historical Theology, Oxford, 1905.

PETERSON, E., "Das Praescriptum des 1 Clemens," *Pro Regno Pro Sanctuario . . . G. van der Leeuw* (Nijkerk, 1950), 351-357.

°SANDERS, L., *L'hellénisme de S. Clément de Rome et le paulinisme.* Louvain, 1943.

SMITH, M., "The Report About Peter in 1 Clement v. 4," *New Testament Studies* 7 (1960-61), 86-88.

TARELLI, C. C., "Clement of Rome and the Fourth Gospel," *Journal of Theological Studies* 48 (1947), 208-209.

°TORRANCE, T. F., *The Doctrine of Grace in the Apostolic Fathers.* Edinburgh, 1948.

VAN UNNIK, W. C., "Is 1 Clement 20 Purely Stoic?" *Vigiliae Christianae* 4 (1950), 181-189.

————, "1 Clement 34 and the 'Sanctus,'" *Vigiliae Christianae* 5 (1951), 204-248.

————, "Zur Bedeutung von 'Tapeinoun tēn psychēn' bei den Apostolischen Vätern," *Zeitschrift für die neutestamentliche Wissenschaft* 44 (1952-53), 250-255.

————, "Le nombre des élus dans la première épître de Clément," *Revue d'histoire et de philosophie religieuses* 42 (1962), 237-246.

WICKERT, U., "Eine Fehlübersetzung zu 1 Clem. 19, 2," *Zeitschrift für die neutestamentliche Wissenschaft* 49 (1958), 270-275.

°WREDE, W., *Untersuchungen zum Ersten Klemensbriefe.* Göttingen, 1891.

°ZIEGLER, A. W., *Neue Studien zum ersten Klemensbrief.* Munich, 1958.

SECOND CLEMENT

SECOND CHAPTER

INTRODUCTION

This sermon, described by its author in 19:1 as an "appeal" (*enteuxis*) dealing to a large extent with "self-control" (15:1), is addressed to a congregation of "brothers and sisters" (19:1; 20:2; cf. 12:5) and probably followed a reading from the scriptures (19:1), perhaps including Isaiah 54:1 (2:1). Its origin is unknown, although it was apparently ascribed to Clement of Rome as early as the third century, for Eusebius, writing early in the fourth century, seems to reject this ascription. Later on, Monophysites—who viewed Jesus Christ as God (1:1)—accepted it as Clement's. What it shares with 1 Clement can be explained as due to a common environment in the Hellenistic Jewish Christianity of the Roman church; the parallels between it and the Shepherd of Hermas are striking. A Roman origin would explain why it was ascribed to Clement and why it makes use of apocryphal materials later employed by Gnostics; it might come from a time when Gnosticism was not yet recognized as dangerous at Rome—perhaps in the time of Hyginus (*ca.* 136–140). Its author was a reader (19:1), probably not in any technical sense; he was probably also one of the presbyters (17:3) who, according to Hermas (Vis. 2, 4, 3), governed the Roman church.

The preacher is no theologian, as his efforts in chapters 9 and 14 make clear. He is, instead, intensely practical, and insists upon repentance as expressed in self-control, abstinence and continence, and in good works. Indeed, he argues (16:4) that almsgiving is better than fasting, which is better than prayer, which is more important than love. This statement goes well beyond what is said in the Jewish apocryphal book of Tobit (12:8–9). Even if one does not

accept the major Pauline epistles as normative, it is difficult
to disagree with Bultmann's statement (II, 171) that the
Christianity of 2 Clement is legalistic and is also influenced
by "certain Hellenistic tendencies of asceticism and flight
from the world."

Indeed, the author has to explain to his hearers why they
should not grieve when they see the unrighteous becoming
rich; if God paid the righteous immediately, they would be
pursuing not piety but profit—in the form of short-term
capital gains (20:1–4). The idea that they are pursuing
profit is encouraged by five references to compensation
(*antimisthia*; only here among the Apostolic Fathers; in a
bad sense in Rom. 1:27) and seven to reward (*misthos*).
In 2 Clement 1:5, indeed, the two words are used together.
Moreover, as Bultmann points out, the author assures his
hearers that, after all, their sojourning in the flesh—before
they receive the reward—will not last long (5:5; 6:6; 7:1;
19:3). One can view this kind of teaching as a crude form
of what is encountered in the Synoptic Gospels (cf. A. N.
Wilder, *Eschatology and Ethics in the Teaching of Jesus*,
rev. ed. [New York, 1950]); more historically, one can suggest that the circumstances in which the sermon was
preached made such a presentation necessary. It may be
that admonitions like those in the letter of James, 1 Clement, Hermas, and even in Ignatius (Smyrn. 6:2) were required—not an emphasis on Pauline teaching such as we
find among the Gnostics.

As a sermon, we may add, 2 Clement lacks the rhetorical
and logical skill evidenced in Hebrews or in the paschal
homily of Melito of Sardis. The preacher proceeds from one
thing to another simply by the association of ideas, sometimes by verbal association. Repentance is a central theme
in chapters 8–18, but there is no clear logical development.

The importance of the work lies simply in its reflection of
rather ordinary Christian (essentially Jewish-Christian) life
and thought in the early second century.

OUTLINE

I. God's gracious, creative action in Christ on our behalf (1:1–2:7)
II. The response of acknowledging him in deed (3:1–4:5)
III. The Christian warfare in this world (5:1–7:6)
IV. Repentance in expectation of the world to come (8:1–12:6)
V. Repentance and faithful obedience in gratitude and in hope (13:1–15:5)
VI. While we have time, then, let us repent, using present opportunities to prepare for the judgment to come (16:1–20:5)

Second Clement

I. God's gracious, creative action in Christ on our behalf (1:1–2:7)

1 Brethren, we ought to think of Jesus Christ just as we do of God, as the Judge of the living and the dead; nor ought we to belittle our salvation. 2. For when we think little of him, we also hope to receive but little. As those who listen as if to a trifling matter sin, so do we when we do not recognize from what and by whom and into what we were called, and how much suffering Jesus Christ endured for us. 3. What repayment, then, can we make to him, or what result commensurate with what he has given us? How many are the blessings we owe to him? 4. For he has given us light; as a Father he has called us

---

1:1–8. The opening verse contains by implication a summary of the homily. It is to deal with the creative act of God or of Christ—and we are to think of the latter as of the former—in making us his people, with judgment, and with salvation. Further, the first chapter exemplifies a leading characteristic of the author's thinking: it is saturated with scripture. Citations are numerous enough: echoes and allusions abound so that at many, many points numerous passages of scripture are suggested. Verses 3 and 5, for example, may remind one of Psalm 115:12; verse 4 of 2 Corinthians 4:6 and Romans 8 or of Hosea 2:1 and 2 Corinthians 6:18; verse 6 of Isaiah 2:8 or Jeremiah 1:16; verses 7 and 8 of 1 Peter 2:9 and 1 Corinthians 1:28.

The opening verse is of course a Christological statement (Lightfoot p. 211), but that is not its function. It is rather programmatic of the whole and a suitable beginning for a chapter whose function in turn is both to commence and to provide a basis for the exhortation by reminding the hearers of what God has freely done for us in Christ. The first verse and the concluding doxology state the high

sons; he rescued us when we were perishing. 5. What praise
then shall we give him or what payment as a return for what
we have received? 6. Our minds were blinded; we worshiped
stone and wood and gold and silver and brass, the works of
men; and our whole life was nothing else but death. And when
we were thus enveloped in darkness and our eyes were so full
of mist, our sight was restored by his will and we laid aside the
cloud that enshrouded us. 7. For he had mercy upon us and in
his compassion saved us, since he saw in us such great deception and destruction and knew we had no hope of salvation unless it came from him. 8. For he called us from nothingness and
willed us into being from nothingness.

2 "Rejoice, O barren one that dost not bear; break forth and
shout, thou who didst not travail; for the desolate hath more
children than she who hath a husband" [Isa. 54:1; Gal. 4:27].
Now when he says, "Rejoice O barren one that dost not bear,"
he refers to us, for our Church was barren before it was given
children. 2. And when he says, "Shout, thou who didst not
travail," he means this: we must not be afraid, like a woman in
travail, but offer our prayers simply and openly before God.

Christology; all between has to do with consequences. This is in
harmony with a fundamental pattern of thought in Old and New
Testament: compare Deuteronomy 5:6 ff. and John 3:16, and the
treatment in C. H. Dodd, *Gospel and Law* (New York, 1951), 10 ff.;
71 ff. Compare also Ignatius, Ephesians 2:2: "It is suitable in every
way to glorify Jesus Christ, who glorified you." For the questions
"whence," "by whom," see commentary on 1 Clement 38:3–4. God's
(Christ's) calling the nonexistent is based on Romans 4:17.

2:1–7. The Scriptures which testify to God's gracious action in
calling us into being also bid us wonder and rejoice. Isaiah 54:1 is
interpreted as applying to Gentiles, just as it is in Justin, *Apology*
I 53 (where it is followed by an allusion to worshiping the work
of men's hands—cf. 1:6 above). Paul used it otherwise in Galatians
4:27. Justin also affirms (*ibid.*) that Gentiles are greater in number
(vs. 3). On the contrast between the Church and Judaism, see
Windisch p. 130. The Church is not the local community but the universal one, as in chapter 14. For the expression "great and wondrous"
see also 5:5 and 1 Clement 26:1 with commentary. For "that which
is lost" (Luke 19:10) 2 Clement substitutes a more explicit (Pauline)
reference to those who were perishing (cf. 1 Cor. 1:18; 2 Cor. 2:15;
4:3; 2 Thess. 2:10); see also 1:4.

3. And he says, "The desolate hath more children than she who hath a husband," since our people seemed to be abandoned by God, but now that we have believed, we have become more numerous than those who seemed to have God. 4. Thus another passage in scripture says, "I did not come to call the righteous, but sinners" [Matt. 9:13 and parallels]. 5. This means that he must save the perishing. 6. For that is the great and wondrous thing, to strengthen not what is standing, but what is fallen. 7. Thus it was that Christ willed to save what was perishing, and he saved many when he came and called us who were already perishing.

II. The response of acknowledging him in deed (3:1–4:5)

3 Since he has shown us such mercy, to begin with in that we who are living do not sacrifice to dead gods nor worship them, but through him have come to know the Father of truth, what is knowledge with reference to him save refusing to deny him

---

3:1–5. The acknowledgment of God is the only appropriate response. The phrase "dead gods" is approximated in the "dead idols" and "dead images" of Wisdom 15:5, 8, 15–17 (see Did. 6:3). "Knowledge with reference to" (*pros*) him is unusual. A.-G. 163 take it as equivalent to an objective genitive; the use of *pros* with verbs meaning to pray, or its use to indicate presence are alternatives. The wording of the quotation in verse 4 follows that of the Gospels; as is the case with that in verse 5, which is quoted in the same form in 1 Clement 15:2.

There may be an anti-Gnostic note in the words about "knowledge" (*gnosis*) in regard to the "Father of truth," for this appellation of God occurs in Valentinian writings. Probably, however, Christians both Gnostic and non-Gnostic used it before it became a Gnostic favorite (cf. 20:5). Honoring God not only with one's lips but "from the whole heart and from the whole understanding" recalls the version of the *Shema* (Deut. 6:5) provided in Mark 12:30 (cf. Matt. 22:37; Luke 10:27). In 2 Clement the words "with all our heart" recur in 17:7 (serve God) and 8:2; 17:1; and 19:1 (repent); "wholehearted repentance" is found in 13:1. It would appear that the author is well acquainted with Jesus' summary of the Law. Deeds are contrasted with words not only here but also in 4:1–2; 9:10; and 13:3.

through whom we came to know the Father? 2. He himself says, "He who acknowledges me before men, I also will acknowledge before my Father" [Matt. 10:32; Luke 12:8]. 3. This then is our reward if only we acknowledge him through whom we were saved. 4. But in what way do we acknowledge him? By doing what he says and not disobeying his commandments, and by honoring him not only with our lips but "with all our heart and all our mind" [Deut. 6:5; Mark 12:30 and parallels]. 5. For he also says in Isaiah, "This people honors me with their lips, but their heart is far from me" [Isa. 29:13; Matt. 15:8; Mark 7:6].

4 Let us not then merely call him Lord, for this will not save us. 2. For he says, "Not every one that says to me, 'Lord, Lord,' will be saved, but he who does righteousness" [Matt. 7:21 and parallels]. 3. So then, brethren, let us acknowledge him in deeds —by loving one another, by refraining from adultery and slander and jealousy, being instead self-controlled, merciful, kind. We ought also to share each other's lot and not be avaricious. In

---

4:1–5. True acknowledgment of God consists in keeping his commandments. "Self-controlled" (vs. 3) may be especially used with reference to matters of sex, as in 15:1; Polycarp 4:2; Hermas, Mandates 8, 1; so here in parallel with *moichasthai* (see further under ch. 15). Verse 4 is an echo of Matthew 10:28. The quotation in verse 5 may be from the Gospel of the Egyptians (Lightfoot p. 218; see the reference to the discussion in Schneemelcher in connection with 12:1–2 below). Schneemelcher says that in this case "extra-canonical tradition must indeed be assumed, but the source must have been very similar to the Synoptic tradition," and "the altered form of these passages" in Justin, *Apology* 1, 16, 11 and *Dialogue* 66, 5 "cannot be drawn upon in explanation." The Gospel parallels are as follows (translated to bring out the parallel words):

Not everyone who says to me, "Lord, Lord," will be saved, but he who performs righteousness.	Not everyone who says to me, "Lord, Lord," will enter the kingdom of heaven, but he who performs the will . . . (Matt. 7:21).
Depart from me; I do not know whence you are, workers of lawlessness.	Depart from me; (Luke 13:27) I do not know whence you are, workers of lawlessness" (Luke 13:27).

The most difficult feature to explain is that Luke 13:27 is parallel to

behavior of that kind and not its opposite we acknowledge him.
4. Further, we must fear not men but God. 5. That is why, assuming you do these things, the Lord said, "Even if you are
with me, gathered to my bosom, but keep not my commandments, I shall cast you out and I shall say to you, 'Go from me,
I do not know you nor whence you are, you workers of iniquity'"
[see commentary].

III. The Christian warfare in this world (5:1–7:6)

5 Wherefore, brethren, having given up in principle our stay
in the strange land of this world, let us do the will of him who
has called us, nor fear to leave this world. 2. For the Lord says
you shall be "as lambs among wolves" [Luke 10:3]. 3. But Peter
answered and said to him, "What if the wolves tear the lambs
to pieces?" 4. Jesus said to Peter, "Let the lambs have no fear
of the wolves after their death, nor are you to fear those who
when they have killed you have no more power over you, but

Matthew 7:22. Why did 2 Clement pass from one Gospel to another?
Or was he relying on oral tradition at this point?
    5:1–7. Our sojourn here is brief, and since this world is not to be
compared with the next, we must use it to gain the latter. The
phraseology "our stay . . . this world" is found in an inscription noted
in A.-G. 634; Philo, *De Confusione Linguarum* 80; *en sōmati paroikia*.
The statement is one of the author's summarizing ones (Windisch p.
123), combining several themes, for example, the rest promised in
Matthew 11:28 and the heavenly rest of Hebrews 3:1–4:13. That
the "rest" promised in Matthew 11:28 is in mind is shown by the
frequent references (such as the one in 6:7) to the commandments
(or will) of Christ. The snatch of dialogue in verses 3–4 is discussed
in Schneemelcher p. 172, who declines to assign it to the Gospel of
the Egyptians. Despite its reminiscences of Matthew 10:6; 10:29, and
parallels (as well as Justin, *Apology* 1, 19, 7; Clement of Alexandria,
Exc. ex Theod. 14, 3 and 51, 3; Irenaeus, *Adv. haer.* 3, 19, 4), he
argues that the form of the dialogue points to a special tradition.
For "great and wondrous" see 2:6 and commentary. For the connection of "rest" with "kingdom" see the Gospel of Thomas (saying 2)
and the parallels cited in R. M. Grant, D. N. Freedman, and W. R.
Schoedel, *The Secret Sayings of Jesus* (Garden City, N.Y., 1960), 120.

fear him who after your death has power over soul and body
to cast into the hell of fire" [cf. Luke 12:4–5; Matt. 10:28]. 5.
You must realize, brethren, that our stay in this world of the
flesh is slight and short, but the promise of Christ is great and
wondrous, even rest in the kingdom to come and in life eternal.
6. What then must we do to attain this, except to lead a godly
and righteous life and to regard the things of this world as alien
to us and not set our hearts upon them? 7. For in setting our
hearts on acquiring these things we fall away from the right
way.

6 The Lord says, "No servant can serve two masters" [Luke
16:13; Matt. 6:24]. If we desire to serve both God and mammon,
it will do us no good. 2. "For what profit is it if a man gain the
whole world but loses his life?" [Matt. 16:26; Luke 9:25.] 3.
This world and the one to come are two enemies. 4. This one
means adultery, corruption, greed, deceit; that one renounces
these things. 5. We cannot therefore be friends of both; we have
to renounce the one to obtain the other. 6. We think it is better
to hate what is here, because it is meager and short-lived and
perishable, and to love what is there, the good and the im-
perishable. 7. For if we do the will of Christ we shall find rest
[cf. Matt. 11:29]; but if not, if we disregard his commandments,

---

6:1–9. One cannot serve both this world and the world to come,
for they are enemies. The thought summarized in verse 2 is encountered with variations in all parts of the New Testament, as, for
example, in Mark 4:19; Matthew 13:32; Galatians 1:4; Ephesians
2:2, 7; 1 Timothy 6:17; Hebrews and the Johannine literature. Here
the opposition is so sharpened or simplified that there is no suggestion
(as in Romans) of living in this age in the transforming power of the
age to come. Otherwise the thought of the two aeons is much like
the Pauline anthesis of flesh-Spirit in Galatians 5 or the aeons of
Adam and of Christ summarized in Romans 5:12–21. Lightfoot p. 221
is mistaken in saying that the word *apotassesthai* ("renounce") is
common in the New Testament: it occurs but six times. Verse 8 contains a characteristically abridged citation from Ezekiel; another idea
borrowed from him (but probably by way of 1 Timothy) is relied
upon in chapter 10. On the reference to "baptism" in verse 9, see the
commentary on 7:6. The last sentence of the verse reproduces the
thought of 2 Esdras 7:102–106, and may be taken as an echo thereof
if that book is thought to be in reference in chapter 17.

nothing will deliver us from eternal punishment. 8. So also the
scripture says in Ezekiel, "Even if Noah, Job, and Daniel were
to rise, they could not deliver their descendants" in the captivity [Ezek. 14:14–20, summarized]. 9. If even such righteous
men are unable by their righteousness to save their descendants,
what assurance have we, if we fail to keep our baptism pure
and undefiled, that we shall enter into the kingdom of God? Or
who will be our advocate, if we are not found to have holy and
righteous deeds?

7 So then, my brethren, let us become contestants, knowing
that the contest is at hand; and knowing also that though many
enter the worldly competitions, not all are crowned but only
those who have worked hard and competed well. 2. Let us then
so compete that we may all be crowned. 3. So let us run a
straight course, the heavenly contest, and let many of us enter
and compete that we also may be crowned; and if we cannot all
win the crown, let us at least come near it. 4. We must bear in
mind that if a contestant in a worldly contest is caught cheating,
he gets a flogging and is thrown out of the stadium. 5. What do
you think? What will be done to the man who cheats in the

7:1–6. Our time in this world, then, is to be used in competing
for the heavenly prize. For the translation "enter . . . competitions," see
A.-G. 417b, with references. The first two sentences probably echo
1 Corinthians 9:24–25, though of course if an analogy drawn from
the Isthmian (?) games is to be used, such language will naturally
occur. The language is reminiscent also of Hebrews 12:1, where the
verb is the more usual *trechōmen* instead of *theōmen* (verse 3). The
figure of the goal recurs in 19:1; the thought of at least coming near
the mark in 18:2 (Lightfoot p. 225 finds references to second or
third prizes in a foot race doubtful). On "cheating" see 2 Timothy
2:5 and Lightfoot's note *ad loc.* The "seal" of verse 6 is the seal of
baptism (cf. 6:9; 8:6; 14:3–5; 16:3–4), as is pointed out by Lightfoot *ad loc.* G. W. H. Lampe, *The Seal of the Spirit* (London, 1951),
103 ff., discusses all the references in 2 Clement. His view is that the
equation of baptism with the seal is "a not unnatural extension of St.
Paul's conception," that it has come to be regarded as primarily con-
nected with the flesh, and that ethical conduct is here as later what
keeps the seal—now thought of metaphorically—inviolate or un-
broken, "so that the flesh, being joined to the Spirit, will ultimately
be able to partake of life and immortality." See also A. Benoit, *Le
baptême chrétien au second siècle* (Paris, 1953), 95–114.

contest for what is incorruptible? 6. For of those who have not kept the seal, it says, "Their worm shall not die and their fire shall not be quenched, and they shall be a spectacle for all flesh" [Isa. 66:24; Mark 9:44, 48].

IV. Repentance in expectation of the world to come (8:1–12:6)

8 So while we are on earth, let us repent. 2. For we are clay in the hand of the craftsman. It is like a potter making a vessel: if it becomes misshapen or breaks in his hands, he molds it again; but if he has already put it into the kiln, he can no longer repair it. So it is with us [cf. Jer. 18:4–6; Rom. 9:19–21]. While we are in this world, let us repent with all our hearts of the evil we have done in the flesh in order that we may be saved by the Lord while we still have opportunity to repent. 3. For after we have passed out of this world we shall no longer be able in the

---

8:1–6. Repentance, resulting in keeping the flesh pure, is required if we are to receive eternal life. The figure of the potter and his clay is derived from Jeremiah 18:4–6; our author adds the idea that the vessel once in the oven cannot be refashioned. On wholehearted repentance see commentary on chapter 3. The idea that no further repentance is possible in the other world seems to be based on the parable of Dives and Lazarus (Luke 16:19–31), especially its ending; but since the parable reflects ordinary Jewish teaching there may be no precise reference (see, however, 2 Clem. 10:4; 11:4). The expression to "keep oneself pure" (hagnon) occurs in 1 Timothy 5:22, and keeping the flesh pure (hagnēn) is in the Acts of Paul and Thecla 5; 12 (cf. Krüger pp. 432–436). Similar counsel, with different but analogous adjectives, is to be found in Hermas, Similitudes 5, 6, 7; 5, 7, 1. Keeping the flesh pure results in obtaining eternal life only in the sense that such purity is the consequence of doing the Father's will. The saying of the Lord consists of a question vaguely resembling a statement in the parable of the talents (Matt. 25:21, 23) and a pronouncement exactly paralleled in Luke 16:10. The contrast between small and great has already been implied in 1:1 and explicitly stated in 5:5; our author explains that the "little" is earthly life (as in 6:6) while what is "great" or "much" is eternal life. He repeats the injunction to keep the flesh pure and adds a mention of preserving the seal (of baptism, cf. 6:9) undefiled; see also 9:3.

next either to confess or to repent. 4. So, brethren, if we do the will of the Father and keep the flesh pure and keep the commandments of the Lord, we shall receive eternal life. 5. For the Lord says in the gospel, "If you fail to guard what is small, who will give you what is great? [cf. Luke 16:11–12]. For I say to you, He who is faithful in a very little is faithful also in much" [Luke 16:10]. 6. What he means, then, is this: keep the flesh pure and the seal undefiled, so that we may receive eternal life.

9 Further, let none of you say that this flesh is not judged nor does it rise again. 2. Consider: in what state were you saved, in what state did you regain your sight, if it was not in this flesh? 3. Hence it is necessary to guard the flesh as the temple of God. 4. For as in the flesh you were called, in the flesh you will come. 5. If Christ the Lord who saved us was first spirit but became

---

9:1–11. The necessity of guarding the flesh in purity is obvious in view of the resurrection. Lightfoot p. 229 compares Hermas, Similitudes 5, 7, 1–2. "Guard this flesh of yours pure and undefiled, so that the spirit which dwells in it may bear it witness and your flesh may be vindicated. . . . For if you defile your flesh you also defile the Holy Spirit, and if you defile the flesh you will not live." The idea of guarding the flesh as a temple of God is also found in the Acts of Paul and Thecla 5, and more exactly in Ignatius, Philadelphians 7:2. Paul uses a similar figure in 1 Corinthians 3:16–17 and 6:19, although he uses the term "body" rather than "flesh"; the second-century emphasis on "flesh" (contrast 1 Cor. 15:44, 50) is probably due in part to the rise of Gnostic "spirituality." To confirm his point, 2 Clement adduces the example of Christ, who was originally "spirit" (cf. 2 Cor. 3:17[?]) but "became flesh" (John 1:14). The idea seems to be related to the obscure Christology reflected in Hermas, Similitudes 5, 6, 5 ("God made the pre-existent Holy Spirit . . . dwell in flesh") or 9, 1, 1 ("the Holy Spirit . . . is the Son of God"). His incarnation implies our carnal resurrection. (See also commentary on ch. 14.) Consequently we should "love one another"—a phrase common in the Johannine writings, but also Pauline (Rom. 13:8; 1 Thess. 4:9)—and, by implication, keep the other commandments. Our author now tries to combine ideas about predestination and free will in a rather confused manner. God heals, saves, calls us sons (1:4). He recognizes us in advance (cf. Rom. 8:29). Yet we owe him a reward or "fee" (1:3, 5; 9:7; 15:2)—repentance expressed not only in word but also in deed (3:4). Doing the will of the Father is set forth in a saying of the Lord roughly parallel to Matthew 12:50, perhaps mixed with Luke 8:21.

flesh and in that state called us, so we also shall receive our reward in this flesh. 6. Let us therefore love one another, so that
we may all enter the kingdom of God. 7. While we have opportunity to be healed, let us entrust ourselves to God the
Physician, and pay him his fee. 8. What fee? The repentance of
a sincere heart. 9. For he foreknows all things and knows what
is in our hearts. 10. Let us then give him praise, not with our
lips only, but with our hearts, that he may receive us as sons.
11. For the Lord said, "My brethren are those who do the will
of my Father" [Matt. 12:50; Luke 8:21; also Mark 3:35].

10 So then, my brethren, let us do the will of the Father who
called us, that we may live; and let our preference be the pursuit of virtue. Let us abandon evil, as the forerunner of our sins,
and flee ungodliness, lest evils overtake us. 2. For if we are eager
to do good, peace will ensue for us [cf. Ps. 33:15]. 3. For the
reason some do not find peace is that they give way to human
fears and prefer pleasures here to what is promised for the
future. 4. They do not know what great torment the pleasures
of the present bring, and what delight the promise of the future.

10:1–5. So let us resolutely turn our backs on evil and give ourselves to the pursuit of the good. *Aretē* in the sense of "virtue" is
found but twice in the New Testament (Phil. 4:8 and 2 Pet. 1:5). It
is of course a great word in Greek *paideia*, and the use óf *diōkein*
suggests that tradition (see W. Jaeger, *Paideia* [New York, 1945],
passim); but our author makes nothing of it except to mention *kakia*
(evil disposition), its opposite. This is in accord with the New Testament: "The word did not suit the intentions of the first Christian
writers" (H. Jonas, *The Gnostic Religion* [Boston, 1958] 155, n. 3.
See also his discussion of *aretē* in *Gnosis und spätantiker Geist*
[Göttingen, 1954], II, 26 ff.). Rather, he turns in the succeeding
verse to a summary of the thought of Psalm 33:11–14, already
drawn upon for similar purposes in 1 Peter 3:10–12 (on the use of
this psalm, see C. H. Dodd, *According to the Scriptures* [New York,
1953], 98–99). The text of verse 3 is corrupt: see the discussion in
Lightfoot pp. 232–234; for the thought see Luke 16:25. The verb
"to teach evil" occurs only here in the New Testament and early
Christian literature; the noun "teachers of evil" is in Titus 2:3. Verse
5 seems to echo or to be tangential to the idea found in three
passages: Matthew 18:6 (causing little ones to sin), Romans 1:32
(doing evil and approving those who do it), and Ezekiel 3:18 and
33:8 (prophet and sinner both to suffer).

5. If they alone did these things, it might be bearable; but as it is, they keep teaching evil to innocent souls, unaware that they will receive a double sentence, both they and those who heed them.

11 Let us then serve God with a pure heart and we shall be righteous. But if, because we do not believe the promise of God, we do not serve him, we shall be wretched. 2. For the prophetic word says, "Wretched are the double-minded, who doubt in their heart and say, 'We heard those things long ago, even in the time of our fathers, and awaiting them day by day we have seen none of them.' 3. Foolish men! Compare yourselves to a tree; take the vine; first it sheds its leaves, then there comes a bud, after this the unripe grape, then the full bunch. 4. So also my people has had tumults and tribulations; later it will receive good things" [cf. 1 Clem. 23:3–4]. 5. So then, my brethren, let

---

11:1–7. If we are to be acceptable with God and enter his kingdom, we must remain steadfast in hope, believing firmly in the promises. The reference to the pure heart (cf. Matt. 5:8; 1 Tim. 1:5; 2 Tim. 2:22) seems to provide a connection by contrast with the end of the preceding chapter, but in fact purity of heart is defined here (vss. 1, 2, 5–6) as hope fixed without wavering on the promises of God. Schneemelcher p. 173 does not think it possible to identify the source of the quotation in verses 2 ff., used both in 1 Clement 23 (see commentary) and here. Verse 4 is reminiscent of the words of Abraham to Dives in Luke 16:25. Doubtless the term "double-minded" in verse 5 comes from the quotation above, but we may note that it is used in the context of the Christian hope in James 1:7 (cf. vs. 2) and in that of wretchedness in James 4:8–9 (cf. vss. 1–2). Verse 7 is cited by G. W. H. Lampe (*The Seal of the Spirit* [London, 1951], 100) in his evaluation of our period in which new converts tended toward an antinomian version of Paulinism or "a relapse into a Judaistic religion of moralism where salvation was once again to be won by human effort, *the Kingdom of God was to be gained by merit,* and a simple untheological monotheism found it exceedingly difficult to accommodate within its narrow system of thought the experience of Christ as God" (italics mine). This is not entirely just if applied to our author, for he is equally emphatic in chapters 1–2 on the point that the Lord has saved us as he is here in his insistence on fidelity (also 3:3; 9:2, 5); and indeed the same flat contradiction, if it is that, is found in Paul in Philippians 2:12–13. For the description of the good things to come see 14:5 and 1 Clement 34:8 (with commentary).

us not be double-minded but remain steadfast in hope, that we may also receive the reward. 6. For "faithful is he who promised" [Heb. 10:23] to pay to each man the wages due for his work [cf. Matt. 16:27; Rom. 2:6; Rev. 2:23]. 7. If then we do what is righteous before God, we shall enter his kingdom and receive the promises "which ear has not heard nor eye seen, nor has entered into the heart of man" [1 Cor. 2:9; cf. Isa. 64:4; 65:16].

12 Let us then be on the watch hour by hour for the kingdom of God, in love and in righteousness, since we do not know the day when the Lord will appear. 2. For the Lord himself, when asked by someone when the kingdom was going to come, said, "When the two are one, and the outside as the inside, and the male with the female, neither male nor female" [cf. Gospel of the Egyptians; Clement of Alexandria *Str.* 3, 92]. 3. Now "the two are one" when we speak the truth among ourselves and two bodies are of one mind with no deception. 4. And "the outside as the inside" signifies this: the "inside" means the soul and the "outside" means the body. Just as your body is visible, so let your soul be manifest in good works. 5. And "the male with the female, neither male nor female" means this: when a brother sees a sister, he is not to think of her sex, nor should she give any

---

12:1–6. Since we have the promise, we are to be on the watch for the kingdom, knowing that when we are sufficiently purified, it will come. The opening verse echoes the sayings on watchfulness in the Gospels, especially Mark 13 and parallels. The phrase *epiphaneia tou theou* is found in the New Testament only in the Pastorals (1 Tim. 6:14; 2 Tim. 1:10; 4:1, 8; Tit. 2:13). The first noun occurs with *tēs parousias* in 2 Thessalonians 2:8. The assignment of the quotation in verse 2 to the Gospel of the Egyptians (despite differences in wording from the similar quotation assigned thereto by Clement of Alexandria) is accepted by Schneemelcher p. 169 and by H. Leisegang (*Die Gnosis*, 4th ed. [Stuttgart, 1955], 135), but van Unnik thinks it extremely doubtful since "the passages they (Clem. Alex., Hippolytus) quote from it do not occur in the work which bears that title in our collection" (W. C. van Unnik, *Newly Discovered Gnostic Writings* [London, 1960], 19). R. M. Grant discusses the passage in *Gnosticism and Early Christianity* (New York, 1959), 123–124. G. F. Moore suggests that it might be Jewish in origin; cf. *Judaism* (Cambridge, Mass., 1927–1930), II, 191; III, 190.

thought to his. 6. When you do these things, he says, the kingdom of my Father will come.

V. Repentance and faithful obedience in gratitude and in hope (13:1–15:5)

13 Therefore, brethren, let us now at last repent and take sober thought for what is good; for we are full of much folly and evil. We must remove our former sins from ourselves and by wholehearted repentance be saved. Let us not seek to please men, nor yet please ourselves only; yet we must commend ourselves to outsiders in righteousness, lest the name be blasphemed on account of us [Ps. 52:5; Eph. 6:6 (?); Rom. 2:24 = Isa. 52:5]. 2. For the Lord says, "My name is continually blasphemed among all the Gentiles" [Isa. 52:5], and again, "Woe to him through whom my name is blasphemed." In what is it blasphemed? In your failure to do what I desire. 3. For when they hear from our lips the oracles of God, they marvel at their beauty and greatness. But then when they observe that our actions are unworthy of the words we utter, they turn to blasphemy, saying that it is a myth and a deception. 4. For when they hear from us that God says, "It is no credit to you if you love those who

---

13:1–4. Thoroughgoing repentance should keep us from conduct that brings the name of God into disrepute. The verb "to take sober thought" occurs in 2 Timothy 2:26 and 1 Peter 4:7; the language suggests an exhortation to a drunken man to "sober up." To do so is regarded as a simple possibility, as Windisch points out. The sanction of earning the respect of outsiders is especially prominent in 1 Peter 2:11–4:11 and is frequent elsewhere in the New Testament letters (e.g., 1 Thess. 4:12; Col. 4:5). The source of the second quotation in verse 2 is not known, unless it is simply an adaptation in free quotation of the first (Lightfoot p. 242). The concern lest the name be blasphemed is a prime sanction in the Old Testament, especially the Second Isaiah and Ezekiel. The "oracles of God" here means the New Testament scriptures, as in 1 Clement 19:1; 53:1; 62:3. The word "myth" is used in verse 3 in the ancient sense—that is, a story that is not true. The Gospel sayings are ascribed to God because of the doctrine set forth in 1:1.

love you, but it is a credit to you if you love your enemies and those who hate you" [Luke 6:32, 35]—when they hear these words they marvel greatly at such extraordinary goodness. But when they see that we not only do not love those that hate us but even do not love those that love us, they laugh us to scorn, and the name is blasphemed.

14 So then, brethren, by doing the will of God our Father, we shall belong to the first Church, the spiritual one, which was created before the sun and the moon [cf. Ps. 71:5]. But if we fail to do the will of the Lord, that passage of scripture will apply to us which says, "My house has become a den of robbers" [Jer. 7:11; cf. Matt. 21:13 and parallels]. We must then choose to be of the Church of life in order to be saved. 2. I do not

---

14:1–5. By doing the will of God in the flesh we qualify to belong to the true, spiritual Church and to receive the Spirit. The thought of verse 1 can be derived easily from Ephesians 1:3 ff. (so Lightfoot p. 243), but is easily adapted to Gnostic purposes. The use of the passage from Jeremiah is strained. Note also (and again) the voluntarism of the last sentence. Again in verse 2 the thought of Ephesians has been extended. The phrase "the books and the apostles" has been much discussed. Lightfoot pp. 245–246 regarded it as clear that the phrase means the Old Testament and the apostolic writings of the New Testament, and so it is taken by Richardson p. 199. The matter is discussed by H. Koester, *Synoptische Uberlieferungen bei den Apostolischen Vätern* (Berlin, 1957). On the other hand, C. F. D. Moule (*The Birth of the New Testament* [New York, 1962], 181) takes the position that the Church of the early second century was not that bookish and regards the phrase as equivalent to *ho kyrios kai hoi apostoloi*, the two recognized sources of authority. The translation of the last sentence in verse 2 is literal; Lake p. 151 believes that "both the context and the history of doctrine" require masculine pronouns in the last clause, referring to Christ. Verse 3 is an application of the idea of the union of the Church with Christ. The second clause is explained by the following words about the antitype and the original, on which see Hebrews 9:24 and Lightfoot p. 247. What is then said about flesh and Spirit serves to clarify what is found in chapter 9. But there is still confusion, for the relation of flesh and Spirit is used to represent two different things: (1) the relation of the Church to Christ (vs. 4); and (2) the relation of the earthly Church and Jesus in the flesh to the heavenly Church and the heavenly Christ. For a discussion of the doctrine expressed or implied here, and its peculiarities, see Windisch p. 130. On his view it is a naively realistic idea of

suppose you are unaware that the living "church is the body of Christ" [Eph. 1:22–23; cf. 1 Cor. 12:27; Col. 1:24; Eph. 4:12]; for the Scripture says, "God created man male and female" [Gen. 1:27]. The male is Christ, the female is the Church. Moreover, the books and the apostles declare that the Church belongs not to the present, but existed from the beginning. For she was spiritual, as was also our Jesus, but was made manifest in the last days that she might save us. 3. Now the Church, being spiritual, was made manifest in the flesh of Christ to show us that if any of us guard her in the flesh and it be not corrupted, he will receive her back in the Holy Spirit. For this flesh is the copy of the Spirit. No one who corrupts the copy will receive the original in its place. This, then, is what it means, brethren: guard the flesh, that you may share in the Spirit. 4. If we say that the flesh is the Church and the Spirit is Christ, then he

---

a premundane marriage that leads first to an identification of the Church with the flesh of Christ and then to a comparison of the manifestation of the Church with the incarnation of Christ. For a more positive evaluation which finds in 2 Clement an adumbration of Augustine's development of the doctrine of the Church as the bride of Christ, see C. Chavasse, *The Bride of Christ* (London, 1940), 115–116.

Both Christ and the Church were originally spirit or spiritual; since the spiritual Church, the Church of life, was created before sun and moon (the fourth day of creation, according to Gen. 1:14–19), Christ's origin must have been even earlier. Christ "became flesh" (John 1:14), and his flesh was a copy or "antitype" of the Spirit; in this fashion he called men. Similarly, the Church, Christ's body, was made manifest in the last days in order to save men. She was made manifest in the flesh of Christ. The two are united as Spirit and flesh and as male and female. One must not "corrupt" the Church or the flesh.

It is difficult not to suppose that most of this is exegesis of Ephesians 5:23–32, where Christ's Church is referred to as his body (5:23) or his flesh (5:29), and the story of Adam and Eve is referred to Christ and his Church (5:31–32). Similarly, the idea of not "corrupting" the Church (Christ's bride) is paralleled in 2 Corinthians 11:2–3; and the statement that the Church is not "now" but "from the beginning" (*anōthen*) recalls Paul's contrast between the Jerusalem "now" and the Jerusalem "above" in Galatians 4:25–26. For revelation through the Church, see Ephesians 3:10. It would appear that the author of 2 Clement lives in an environment where imaginative exegesis like that of the Gnostics is already flourishing.

who does violence to the Church does violence to Christ. Such a man will not share in the Spirit, which is the Christ. 5. This flesh is able to receive so great a life and immortality because the Holy Spirit is closely joined to it, nor can·anyone express or declare "what things the Lord has prepared" [1 Cor. 2:9] for his elect.

15 Now I think the advice I have given about self-control is not unimportant, since one who follows it will not regret doing so, but will save both himself and me his counselor [cf. Ezek. 3:21; 1 Tim. 4:16]. For the reward is not small if we turn back to salvation a soul wandering and perishing [cf. Jas. 5:20]. 2. For this is the return we can make to God who created us, if the one who speaks and the one who hears do so with faith and love. 3. Let us then remain holy and righteous in our faith, that we may make our requests with boldness to the God who says, "While you are still speaking, I shall say, Behold, here I am" [Isa. 58:9]. 4. Surely this word is the sign of a great promise; for

---

15:1–5. Self-control is of paramount importance: not only does it bring its reward, but it is also the appropriate expression of gratitude and joy in the Lord. The term self-control (*enkrateia*) plays a restricted role in the thought of the New Testament, in contrast to its prominence in Greek and Hellenistic philosophical ethics (W. Grundmann, *Theologisches Wörterbuch zum Neuen Testament* II, 338–340). In Hellenistic usage it commonly has an ascetic connotation (Encratites), especially with regard to sex (as in 1 Cor. 7:9), but in the New Testament it usually has a more general meaning and is found in combination with other virtues (so Acts 24:25; Gal. 5:23; 2 Pet. 1:6). It is frequent in Hermas (six times) and the adjectival form is his own epithet (Vis. 1, 2, 4). 1 Clement employs it in 35:2; 62:2; ch. 64 (in a list); and in 38:2 speaks of it as bestowed by God. Here it is evidently used as a summary term to gather up what has been said in the preceding chapters about righteous action, guarding the flesh (especially), and so forth.

The transition to verse 2 is mainly verbal (reward-return) but the underlying thought in the chapter is mutuality. The last half of verse 4 is probably an echo of Isaiah 65:1 (cf. Rom. 10:20). Verse 5 is possibly an echo of Mark 16:16; and for the thought, compare Romans 2:6 ff.

There is something of a break between chapters 1–14 and chapters 15–20, and the author seems to indicate this when he says that he has given advice about self-control (15:1). There are some interesting

the Lord declares himself more ready to give than we to ask.
5. Since then we are partakers of such abundant kindness, let us
not begrudge ourselves the gaining of such great benefits. For
these sayings produce for those who do them a joy as great as the
condemnation that falls on those who disregard them.

VI. While we have time, then, let us repent, using present opportunities to prepare for the judgment to come (16:1–20:5)

16 So, brethren, since we have been granted no small opportunity to repent, let us take the occasion to turn to God who
has called us, while we still have one to accept us. 2. For if we
renounce present enjoyments and master our souls by not yielding
to their evil desires, we shall share in Jesus' mercy. 3. Recognize
that "the day" of judgment is already "on its way like a furnace
ablaze" [Mal. 4:1] and some "of the heavens will dissolve" [Isa.
34:4 (?); 2 Pet. 3:12 (?)] and the whole earth will melt like

---

differences in vocabulary which are largely, but not entirely, related
to differences in subject matter.

Chapters 1–14	Chapters 15–20
sarx (flesh); nineteen times	once (17:5); means "mankind"
pneuma (spirit); six times	once (20:4); means "person"
pneumatikos (spiritual); three times	not at all
psychē (soul)	
with body (5:4; 12:3–4)	body not mentioned
good or potentially so (6:2; 10:5; 13:1)	needs to be conquered (16:2)
	perishing (15:1; 17:1); indulgent (17:7)

These differences do not necessarily suggest that 2 Clement consists
of two separate documents, but they may imply that the author later
added chapters 15–20 to his earlier sermon, chapters 1–14.

16:1–4. The imminence of the judgment should stir us to abound
in virtues, turning away from this world and its desires. "Take the
occasion" represents *kairon echontes* (cf. 8:2; 9:7). "Present enjoyments" represents *hēdupatheias*, a term absent from the New Testament and found only here and in 17:7 in early Christian literature. It
was a term of opprobrium among the Stoics and is found in the
heavily Stoic 4 Maccabees 2:2, 4 (see A.-G. p. 345 and Lightfoot p.

lead in a fire; and then the secret and the open works of men will be manifest. 4. Almsgiving, like repentance for sin, is good. Fasting is better than prayer, almsgiving better than both; for "love covers a multitude of sins" [Prov. 10:12; 1 Pet. 4:8], while prayer rising from a clear conscience rescues from death. Blessed is everyone who is found abounding in these; for almsgiving lightens the load of sin.

17 Let us then repent with a whole heart, lest one of us be lost. For if we have a commandment to do this, namely, to draw men away from idolatry and to instruct them, how much more necessary is it that the soul which already knows God should not perish? 2. Let us then help each other to restore especially those who are weak in goodness, so that we may all be saved, both converting and admonishing one another. 3. It is not just that we should appear to believe and to attend now while we

---

250). The words from Isaiah 34 in verse 3 are found in the Septuagint margin in Rahlfs's edition, except for the word *tines*, where Septuagint margin has *pasai*; but the quotation may be in fact an adaptation of 2 Peter 3:12. It may be (Lightfoot p. 251) that the sayings in verse 4 derive from Tobit 12:8, 9, but they could easily be adaptations and summaries of New Testament texts beginning from Matthew 6. *Eleēmonsynē* here means almsgiving, as the last clause shows, reflecting the Jewish doctrine of almsgiving as the great intercessor. That is expressed in Daniel 4:27, which G. F. Moore renders, "Redeem thy sins by almsgiving, and thine iniquity by showing mercy to the poor" (*Judaism*, II, 171; see also pp. 166–173).

17:1–7. Let us practice repentance and mutual strengthening, that we may all be gathered into life on the day of his appearing. The theme of mutuality is continued here and comes to more explicit expression. On "repent with a whole heart," see 8:2 and 19:1. The "commandment" Lightfoot takes to be Matthew 28:19–20, with Mark 16:15 adduced for comparison. But it need not be a specific command. The translation "converting" in verse 2 may be too strong: in 1 Clement 59:4 the verb is used of bringing back those who have gone astray, and that is probably the meaning here. "Admonish" is frequent in the New Testament; with "one another" in Romans 15:4. On the thought of the whole verse, compare 1 Thessalonians 5:14 and Romans 15:1. Verse 3, together with 19:1, indicates the setting of congregational worship in which the word is read and expounded. On this see R. M. Grant, ed., *The Apostolic Fathers* (New York, 1964), Vol. 1, pp. 173 ff. On the exhortation to frequent meeting, compare Hebrews 10:25; Ignatius, Ephesians 13:1; Polycarp 4:2; Didache

are being admonished by the elders: rather, when we have re-
turned home, we should be mindful of the commands of the
Lord and not be drawn away by "worldly desires" [Tit. 2:12],
but try to come here more frequently and make progress in the
commandments of the Lord, that all "with a common mind"
[Rom. 12:16] may be gathered into life. 4. For the Lord said,
"I am coming to gather all nations, peoples, and tongues" [Isa.
66:18; Dan 3:7]. This refers to the day of his appearing, when
he will come to redeem us, each according to his deeds. 5. And
the unbelievers "shall see his glory" [Isa. 66:18] and might, and
they will be astonished to see that sovereignty over the world
belongs to Jesus, and they will say, "Woe is us, for you really
did exist, and we did not know it nor did we believe and obey
the elders who preached to us of our salvation." "And their
worm will not die and their fire will not be quenched, and they
shall be a spectacle to all flesh" [Isa. 66:24; Mark 9:48]. 6. He
means that day of judgment, when men shall see those among
us who were ungodly and perverted the commandments of Jesus
Christ. 7. But the righteous who have done what is right, stead-
fastly endured tortures and hated the pleasures of this life, when
they behold those who have gone astray or denied Jesus either
in word or in deed being punished in dreadful torments and fire
unquenchable, will "give glory to their God" [Ps. 67:35 LXX;
Rev. 11:13(?)] and say, "There is hope for him who has served
God with his whole heart."

18 Let us also then be of the number of those who give thanks
and who have served God, and not of the number of the ungodly who are condemned. 2. For though I myself am utterly
sinful and not yet escaped from temptation but on the contrary
still in the midst of the devil's devices, still I make every effort

---

16:2. The Lord in verse 4 is evidently the Lord Jesus (Harnack,
Windisch, Lightfoot); on "appearing" see under 12:1. On "each according to his deeds," compare 1 Corinthians 3:13 and Romans 2:6;
but "redeem" is not New Testament usage in this context unless here,
as in verse 5, the author is thinking of Revelation. For the thought of
verses 5 ff., compare Matthew 25 and perhaps 2 Esdras 7.

18:1–2.   This chapter is a part of the preceding one, verse 1 carry-
ing forward the picture of the separation at the judgment as in, for
example, Matthew 25 or Revelation 20. Verse 2 is reminiscent of
Philippians 3:12. "The devil's devices" is found only here, but com-

to pursue righteousness to the end that I may be able at least to approach it; for I fear the judgment to come.

19 So, brothers and sisters, following the God of truth [1 Esd. 4:41], I am reading you an appeal to heed the Scriptures, that you may save both yourselves and him who reads in your presence. For I ask as compensation that you repent with your whole heart, granting to yourselves salvation and life. For when we have done so, we shall provide a goal for the young who wish to devote themselves to what concerns piety and the goodness of God. 2. And let us not be so foolish as to be displeased and indignant if anyone admonishes us and turns us from wickedness to righteousness. For sometimes, because of double-mindedness and the unbelief lodged in our hearts, we do what is wrong without knowing it, and "our understanding is darkened" [Eph. 4:17, 18; Rom. 1:21] by vain desires. 3. Let us then do what is right,

---

pare 1 Timothy 3:7 and 2 Timothy 2:26 (the devil's trap), Ignatius, Ephesians 10:3 (ambuscades), Martyrdom of Polycarp 3:1 (machinations). *Panthamartolos* in verse 2 is a *hapax legomenon*. The author associates himself with his hearers even in their sin (cf. 1 Tim. 1:15; Barn. 5:9; also Luke 5:8).

19:1–4. In the light of scriptures and its meaning for us, we should exercise patience in the hope of blessedness. The opening phrase is understood in the light of 13:2, 3; 3:1; and 20:5 to refer to the reading of scripture. Lightfoot cites for comparison Justin, *Apology* 1, 67; Origen, *Contra Celsum* 3, 50 and *Apostolic Constitutions* 2, 54. On the third clause see under 15:1. The second sentence may give support to the conjecture that "double honor" in 1 Timothy 5:17 refers to the payment of elders (among whom our author evidently counts himself in 17:3); and on the necessity for the church of those who could teach and interpret the Scriptures, and the question of their titles, see Ph.-H. Menoud, *L'Église et les ministères* (Neuchâtel, 1949), 35–55. "To devote" themselves (*philoponein*) is classical, found only here in early Christian literature. On verse 2, compare Matthew 18:15–20. The eschatological understanding of salvation is emphasized again in verses 3 and following. The "immortal harvest" is that of which Christ is the first fruits (1 Cor. 15:23). On verse 4, compare Romans 8:18 and James 5:7. "Come to life again" in verse 4 is found only here in early Christian literature (cf. A.-G. 50a). It is found in 2 Maccabees 7:9, whose simple idea of resurrection as resuscitation our author seems to share. For life after death with "the fathers" see Luke 16:23. These fathers are either Jewish or Christian, quite possibly both, as in 1 Clement 23:3; 30:7; 60:4; 62:2; and 2 Clement 11:2.

that we may finally be saved. Blessed are they who obey these injunctions; and if for a little while they suffer in this world [cf. 1 Pet. 5:10], they will gather the immortal harvest of the resurrection. 4. So let not the pious man be grieved if at the present time he is miserable. A time of blessedness awaits him. When he has come to life again with the fathers above, he will rejoice in an eternity that knows no grief.

20 But you must not be troubled in mind by the fact that we see the unrighteous prospering while the servants of God are in straits. 2. We must have faith, brothers and sisters: we are engaging in the contest of the living God, and we are being trained by the present life that we may be crowned by that which is to come. 3. None of the righteous has obtained a reward quickly, but waits for it. 4. For if God were to bestow the reward of the righteous immediately, we should forthwith be training ourselves in commerce and not in godliness; we should give the appearance of being righteous while pursuing in fact not piety but profit. And that is why the divine judgment punishes a spirit when it is not righteous, and loads it with chains.

5. "To the only invisible God" [cf. 1 Tim. 1:17], the Father of truth, who sent to us the Savior and Prince [Acts 5:31] of immortality, through whom also he disclosed to us the truth and heavenly life—to him be glory for ever and ever. Amen.

20:1–5. This life is a time of testing and for the exercise of patience. Glory be to God who has given us a firm ground for hope. Verse 1 expresses a common theme and problem of the Old Testament and of Jewish piety which comes to classical expression in Psalm 73 and is often reflected in the New Testament—for example, in the canticles in Luke or James 5. On verse 2, see chapter 7. Verse 3 may be in a sense a summary of Hebrews 11. On the warning against base motives implicit in the following, compare Matthew 6; though the concluding sentence of verse 4 expresses both in language (*blaptein*) and thought the idea of the divine vengeance as found in Greek classical literature. On this see Lightfoot p. 260, with citations. The language of Jude 6 is similar, but there the reference is not to men but to angels guilty of *hybris*.

The doxology, despite the terminology, expresses again, as did the opening verses of the work, the basically Johannine picture of Christ which our author has carried into his reading and understanding of the Synoptics (Windisch).

QUOTATIONS FROM SCRIPTURE

Passage		2 Clement	Introductory Formula
Gen.	1:27	14:2	for the scripture says
Deut.	6:5; Mark 12:30	3:4	lacking
Isa.	29:13; Matt. 15:8; Mark 7:6	3:5	he [Christ or God] also says in Isaiah
Isa.	34:4(?); 2 Pet. 3:12(?)	16:3	lacking
Isa.	52:5; Rom. 2:24	13:2	for the Lord says
Isa.	54:1; Gal. 4:27	2:1	he says
Isa.	58:9	15:3	God who says
Isa.	66:18; Dan. 3:7	17:4	for the Lord said
Isa.	66:18	17:5	lacking
Isa.	66:24; Mark 9:44, 48	7:6	it says
Isa.	66:18; Mark 9:48	17:5	lacking
Jer.	7:11; Matt. 21:13	14:1	that passage of scripture
Ezek.	14:14–20, summarized	6:8	the scripture says in Ezekiel
Ps.	67:35; Rev. 11:13(?)	17:7	lacking
Prov.	10:12; 1 Pet. 4:8	16:4	lacking
Mal.	4:1	16:3	lacking
Matt.	7:21	4:2	for he [Christ] says
Matt.	9:13	2:4	another passage in scripture says
Matt.	10:32; Luke 12:8	3:2	he himself [Christ] says
Matt.	12:50; Luke 8:21; Mark 3:35	9:11	for the Lord [Christ] said
Matt.	16:26; Luke 9:25	6:2	lacking
Luke	6:32, 35	13:4	God says
Luke	10:3	5:2	for the Lord [Christ] says
Luke	16:10	8:5	for I [the Lord, Christ] say to you
Luke	16:13; Matt. 6:24	6:1	the Lord [Christ] says
Rom.	12:16	17:3	lacking
1 Cor.	2:9	11:7; 14:5	lacking

	Passage	2 Clement	Introductory Formula
Eph.	4:17, 18; Rom. 1:21	19:2	lacking
1 Tim.	1:17	20:5	lacking
Tit.	2:12	17:3	lacking
Heb.	10:23	11:6	lacking

ALLUSIONS TO SCRIPTURE

(The following allusions seem clear; other possible echoes are noted in the commentary.)

Passage	2 Clement	Formula, if any
Isa. 65:1	15:4	
Jer. 18:4–6; Rom. 9:19–21	8:2	
Ezek. 3:18	10:5	
Ezek. 3:21; 1 Tim. 4:16	15:1	
Ezek. 33:8	10:5	
Ps. 33:15	10:2	
Ps. 52:6; Eph. 6:6(?); Rom. 2:24 (Isa. 52:5)	13:1	
Ps. 71:5	14:1	
2 Esdras 7:102–106(?)	6:9	
Matt. 10:28	4:4	
Matt. 11:28	5:5	
Matt. 11:29	6:7	
Matt. 16:27; Rom. 2:6; Rev. 22:16	11:6	
Matt. 18:6	10:5	
Mark 13 par.	12:1	
Mark 16:16	15:5	
Luke 12:4–5; Matt. 10:28	5:4	Jesus said
Luke 16:11–12	8:5	For the Lord says in the gospel
Acts 5:31	20:5	
Rom. 1:32	10:5	
1 Cor. 3:16–17	9:3	
1 Cor. 6:19	9:3	
1 Cor. 9:24–25	7:1–2	

Passage	2 Clement
2 Cor. 3:17(?)	9:5
Eph. 1:22–23; 1 Cor. 12:27; Col. 1:24; Eph. 4:12	14:2
Heb. 3:1–4:13	5:5
1 Pet. 5:10	19:3
2 Pet. 3:12(?)'	16:3
Jas. 5:20	15:1

SELECTED BIBLIOGRAPHY

(Books or articles marked * are usually cited only by the author's name)

BULTMANN, R., *Theology of the New Testament*. 2 vols. New York, 1951, 1955.

CHAVASSE, CLAUDE, *The Bride of Christ. An Enquiry into the Nuptial Element in Early Christianity*. London, 1940.

DODD, C. H., *According to the Scriptures. The Sub-structure of New Testament Theology*. New York, 1953.

——, *Gospel and Law. The Relation of Faith and Ethics in Early Christianity*. New York, 1951.

GRANT, R. M., *Gnosticism and Early Christianity*. New York, 1959.

JAEGER, WERNER, *Paideia: The Ideals of Greek Culture*. 3 vols. New York, 1945 (2d ed.), 1943, 1944.

JONAS, HANS, *Gnosis und spätantiker Geist*. 2 vols. Göttingen, 1954.

——, *The Gnostic Religion. The Message of the Alien God and the Beginnings of Christianity*. Boston, 1958.

KOESTER, HELMUT, *Synoptische Überlieferungen bei den Apostolischen Vätern*. Berlin, 1957.

*KRÜGER, GUSTAV, "Bemerkungen zum zweiten Klemensbrief," in *Studies in Early Christianity*, ed. Shirley Jackson Case. New York, 1928.

*LAKE, KIRSOPP, *The Apostolic Fathers*. Vol. I. London, 1912.

LAMPE, G. W. H., *The Seal of the Spirit. A Study in the Doctrine of Baptism and Confirmation in the New Testament and the Fathers*. London, 1951.

LEISEGANG, HANS, *Die Gnosis*. 4th ed. Stuttgart, 1955.

*LIGHTFOOT, J. B., *The Apostolic Fathers. Part I: S. Clement of Rome*. 2 vols. London, 1890. (Citations are from Vol. II.)

LIPSIUS, R. A., and BONNET, M., *Acta Apostolorum Apocrypha*. 3 vols. Hildesheim, 1959 (photomech. reprod. of ed. of 1891).

MENOUD, Ph.-H., *L'Église et les ministères*. Neuchâtel, 1949.

MOORE, GEORGE FOOT, *Judaism in the First Centuries of the Christian Era. The Age of the Tannaim*. 3 vols. Cambridge, Mass., 1927-1930.

MOULE, C. F. D., *The Birth of the New Testament*. New York, 1962.

*RICHARDSON, C. C., ed., *Early Christian Fathers*. Philadelphia, 1953.

*SCHNEEMELCHER, WILHELM, ed., Edgar Hennecke (earlier ed.), *New Testament Apocrypha*. Eng. trans. by R. McL. Wilson. Volume I. (Gospels and Related Writings.) Philadelphia, 1963.

————, Edgar Hennecke, *Neutestamentliche Apokryphen in deutscher Übersetzung.* Band I, *Evangelien;* Band II, *Apostolisches Apokalypsen und Verwandtes.* Tübingen, 3. Aufl., 1959, 1964.

VAN UNNIK, W. C., *Newly Discovered Gnostic Writings. A Preliminary Survey of the Nag-Hammadi Find.* Studies in Biblical Theology. London, 1960.

*WINDISCH, HANS, "Das Christentum des zweiten Clemensbriefes," in *Harnack-Ehrung: Beiträge zur Kirchengeschichte.* Leipzig, 1921.

A.-G., *A Greek-English Lexicon of the New Testament and Other Early Christian Literature. A translation and adaptation of Walter Bauer's Griechisch-Deutsches Wörterbuch zu den Schriften des Neuen Testaments und der übrigen urchristlichen Literatur* (4th revised and augmented edition, 1952). By William F. Arndt and F. Wilbur Gingrich. Chicago, 1957.